gorse | *Number One*

Published in Dublin in an edition of 350 copies APRIL 2014
of which this is no.

0 2 0 5

gorse | art in words

Copyright © *gorse* and individual contributors, 2014. All rights reserved. No reproduction, copy or transmission, in whole or in part, may be made without written permission.

Published in Dublin January 2014 by *gorse*
ISBN 978-0-9928047-0-1
ISSN 2009-7093

GORSE, NO. 1
www.gorse.ie

EDITORS Susan Tomaselli & David Gavan
COVER ART Niall McCormack | home.hitone.ie

The editors would like to thank David Minogue; Jason Walsh; Therese Murray; Ilya Evkadov; Brian J. Showers; Esther Galfalvi; David Upton at the Project Arts Centre; Magnum Photos.

Contents

EDITORIAL	5	
ESSAYS		
The Magnet has a Soul & Everything is Water, *How modernism is ancient*	11	Darran Anderson
The Run of the Streets	45	Karl Whitney
Appetite for Depletion, *Thoughts on Michel Houellebecq*	97	Rob Doyle
Various Assumptions, *The Still Lives of the Artists*	153	Kevin Breathnach
Close to the Edit, *The Films of Nicolas Roeg*	170	Richard Kovitch
FICTION		
Inverted Yearning	40	Julie Reverb
Killing Off Ray Apada	79	Matthew Jakubowski
Vagues / Прошлым летом на море	124	Joanna Walsh / Anna Aslanyan
Oslo, Norway *An Extract*	183	John Holten
Thornback Ray	224	Desmond Hogan
POETRY		
Six Poems from {Enthusiam}	73	S.J. Fowler
Crocodile	141	Colin Herd
ART		
The Fuse	44	
Isms	72	
A Brand New Axe	114	
Not From Around Here	169	
There Isn't Much Time Now	223	Stephen Crowe

INTERVIEWS
Evan Lavender-Smith 57 David Winters
Adam Thirlwell 115 Susan Tomaselli
Jesse Jones 193 David Gavan

APPENDIX 256

CONTRIBUTORS 257

FRIENDS OF GORSE 260

Editorial
Where the Dead Voices Gather

'Mr Yeats has been speaking to me of your writing…' In December 1913, Ezra Pound[1] wrote to James Joyce asking permission to include a poem of his, 'I Hear an Army,' in the anthology *Des Imagistes*. Joyce, living in self-imposed exile in Trieste and struggling to make ends meet— he had yet to make money from his writing[2]—readily agreed. 'This is the first time I have written to any one outside of my own circle of acquaintance (save in the case of French authors)... I am *bonae voluntatis*—don't in the least know that I can be of any use to you - or you to me. From what W.B.Y. says, I imagine we have a hate or two in common—but thats [*sic*] a very problematical bond on introduction.'

Joyce sent Pound more work, and Pound, drawn to Joyce's tribulations with censorious publishers—it took Joyce almost ten years for *Dubliners* to be published without expurgation—took up the cause. Acting as Joyce's unpaid agent, Pound used his connections as literary correspondent and editor to shepherd *A Portrait of the Artist as a Young Man*—as a serialisation in Harriet Shaw Weaver's *The Egoist* in 1914—and parts of *Ulysses*—first serial publication in *The Little Review* in 1918—into print.

'Enter a skinny, shabby Irishman and a natty, quietly sinister American,' as Kevin Jackson describes them[3], 'hell-bent on exploding everything that realistic fiction and

---

1 *Pound / Joyce: The Letters of Ezra Pound to James Joyce*, ed. Forest Read (New Directions 1967)

2 *Chamber Music* was published in 1907, but the contract required sales 300 for royalties to be paid. It had sold 200. See *Joyce & His Publishers*, Ira B. Nadel (National Library of Joyce Studies 2004)

3 *Constellation of Genius, 1922: Modernism Year One* (Hutchinson 2012)

Georgian poetry held dear ... Language has rebelled against the tyranny of subject matter and character, and become the leading character in its own right. The horror!'

As the 'unconscious mind, like the city, spends its time recycling events,'[4] so too did the moderns reuse the 'debris of previous literature.' Pound and co.—as Darran Anderson discusses in the opening essay[5]—picked up signals from ancient sources, remaking it new.

'I want a place I and T.S. Eliot can appear once a month,' and where Joyce can appear when he likes, and where Wyndham Lewis can appear if he comes back from the war,' writes Pound to *Little Review* editor Margaret Anderson[6] in 1917. Those places, the 'little magazines'—*The Little Review, The Dial, Poetry, Broom, The Egoist* and others—were crucial in getting the work of the 'men of 1914' (as Lewis dubbed himself, Eliot, Pound and Joyce) in print. Often publishing outside of the mainstream and challenging the very notions of what literature could be, they were the perfect venues for the exiles to explore new modes of writing. More significantly, the little magazines welcomed important work other editors had dismissed or ignored. They fast became hotbeds for innovation in new forms: first surrealism, then modernism.

---

4 *Modern Times, Modern Places*, Peter Conrad (Thames & Hudson 1998)

5 'The Magnet has a Soul & Everything is Water: How modernism is ancient,' *gorse*, pages 11-39

6 Quoted in *Eliot, Joyce & Company*, Stanley Sultan (OUP 1990)

Their relationship, though, cooled—Pound had no love[7] for Joyce's new 'Work in Progress,' Joyce was alarmed (and rightly so) at Pound's politics. The reversal of support from a former champion was disappointing, but Joyce was to find other encouragement in American ex-patriates Eugene and Maria Jolas. The Jolas' *transition* journal ran extracts from André Breton's *Nadja* and the surrealist manifesto 'Hands Off Love,' introduced Kafka to an English readership with 'The Sentence' and 'Metamorphosis,' ran dadaist work by Hans Arp and Kurt Schwitters, published bits of Hart Crane's 'The Bridge,' some Gertrude Stein and early Samuel Beckett, and much of *Finnegans Wake* as 'Work in Progress.'

The frontline of the avant-garde in Paris, *transition* was the firecracker the middle class, middlebrow, patrons of the arts needed: their 1929 manifesto[8] was incendiary stuff. It began,

> Tired of the spectacle of short stories, novels, poems and plays still under the hegemony of the banal word, monotonous syntax, static psychology, descriptive naturalism, and desirous of crystallizing a viewpoint...

---

[7] 'Nothing short of divine vision or a new cure for the clapp can possibly be worth all the circumambient peripherization.' *The Letters of Ezra Pound*, quoted in *Transition 1927-38: The History of. Literary Era*, Dougald McMillan (Calder and Boyers 1975). It was a book, Beckett said, 'not about something; it is that something itself.'

[8] 'Manifesto for The Revolution of the Word,' from *transition No. 16-17*, June 1929. The full proclamation can be read at: http://sites.davidson.edu/littlemagazines/transition-manifesto/

We hereby decree that:

1. The Revolution of the English Language is an accomplished fact.
2. The imagination in search of a fabulous world is autonomous and unconfined.
[..]
11. The writer expresses. He does not communicate.
12. The plain reader be damned.

A dismantled syntax, a new multilingual tongue, *transition* was a perfect fit for James Joyce's buckled style. 'The same people,' writes Peter Conrad, 'did not think in paragraphs or logical, completed sentences, like characters in nineteenth-century novels. Their mental life proceeded in associative jerks and spasms… The modern mind was not a quiet, tidy cubicle for cognition. It thronged with as many random happenings as a city street; it contained scraps and fragments, dots and dashes, like the incoherent blizzard of marks on a modern canvas which could only be called an 'impression' because it represented nothing recognizable.'

Joyce, Gertrude Stein and the other *transition* contributors were employing English in radically new ways, bending and regenerating a language made dull by age and usage.[9] 'Joyce,' says Peter Gay,[10] 'pushed the dissection and reconstitution of prose to an extreme that nobody could surpass without

---

9 Turn to 'Speeds & Shapes of Consciousness,' David Winters' and Evan Lavender-Smith's conversation on James Joyce and modernism, on pages 57-71

10 *Modernism: The Lure of Heresy* (William Heinemann 2007)

landing in sheer incoherence.' *Finnegans Wake* could not serve as a novel for later subversive writers, Gay continues, but 'it remains—and will remain—a solitary monument to a bold, learned, and unduplicible venture, serving as Joyce always did to affront dominant literary pieties.'

'In the buginning is the wood, in the muddle is the sound-dance and thereinoften you're in the unbewised again.'

•

One of the finest Irish novels of 2013, Eimear McBride's *A Girl is a Half-Formed Thing*, was ignored for nine years, dismissed as being too experimental. English indie publishers Galley Beggars Press took a punt with it and it went on to win the Goldsmith's Prize, a prize that embraces the enthusiasm of Laurence Sterne—another great Irish innovator—and rewards 'fiction that breaks the mould or opens up new possibilities for the novel form.' Novels that are *novel*.

Another, Donal Ryan's *The Spinning Heart*, a novel in voices, was rejected forty-seven times before being rescued from the 'slush pile' by a beady-eyed intern and published to international acclaim by Irish independents Lilliput Press. They—McBride and Ryan, Galley Beggars and Lilliput—are stories of our time.

Donal Ryan has said we are in the eye of a publishing storm; we think he's on to something. The optimism of the 50's, and the spirit of Ireland's own little magazines—*The Bell, Threshold, Atlantis, The Dublin Magazine*—is alive and well in the *Dublin Review* and *The Stinging Fly*, and in newcomers *The Moth, The Penny Dreadful, South Circular, The Bohemyth*. Though the James Joyces, the Ezra Pounds, the Gertrude Steins, the Ernest Hemingways of today would still be deemed uncommercial (well, perhaps not Hemingway), praise be the independents and the little magazines, for giving voice to innovation, for ushering exciting and unusual authors into print.

For all our talk of the ghosts of Ezra Pound and James Joyce, *gorse* does not wish to raise the dead. We are not nostalgic for the past, but look for the potential in literature today—we believe in the art of words. But we are not only for the *novel*; we champion the unconventional and the under-recognised, writers exiled in their own countries.

'I hear an army charging upon the land…'

The Magnet has a Soul & Everything is Water
How modernism is ancient by Darran Anderson

'On or about December 1910,' Virginia Woolf wrote in her essay *Mr Bennett and Mrs Brown*, 'human character changed.' *Homo modernus* had emerged, like some rough but eloquent beast, in the depths of an English winter. Woolf's perspective of the birth of modernism was subjective of course and the date has been continually disputed. In his recent study, *Constellation of Genius*, Kevin Jackson selected as late as 1922 as 'Modernism Year One.' For many, T.S. Eliot included, the industrialised threshing of an entire generation of European youth by their parents in the Great War of 1914 to 1918 fragmented the old order and created something different, either as a presence or an absence. This was supported by the appearance of dada in the wartime refuge of Zurich; being a wilfully deranged but, to paraphrase R.D. Laing, rational reaction to an insane world. Yet there were identifiable modernists before this—Apollinaire, Marinetti, Jarry—to say nothing of the forerunners of modernism: Nietzsche, Ibsen, Jean-Pierre Brisset, Conrad, Strindberg, Lautréamont, Rimbaud. What becomes clear the further back you go, is this process does not effectively come to a standstill. There is no absolute point of beginning. As a way of looking at the world and recreating it, modernism, meta-modernism, postmodernism and deconstructionism have always been with us, long before we gave them such ludicrous names.

The timing of modernism is important because of the vacuum it's perceived to have left when it dissipated (a likewise disputed period between the World Wars). With commendable intentions, the more adventurous writers today bemoan the fall of the movement and the retreat of much of the literary community into pseudo-Victorian ways of approaching the novel. They discuss its loss with a hint of grief and the desire that it will come again, resurrected to save the day, like millenarian peasants awaiting the Messiah or Jacobites the Young Pretender. Who will save us from ourselves? A more compelling view is that modernism was not entirely obliterated in a collective loss of nerve but survived abroad, in isolated pockets, underground, or flourished in science fiction and comic books. Yet when you begin to list the writers who have reputedly kept the spirit of modernism alive, you find their number is colossal, making up the more critically acclaimed sections of contemporary literature. Indeed, the loss of confidence is not restricted to mainstream novelists. The admirable question posed by Gabriel Josipovici—*What Ever Happened to Modernism?*—has been answered not by polemics but by fiction. It is still there when we search for it.

Modernism didn't disappear because it never definitively appeared. It has been part of our character since at least the earliest identifiable story, the *Epic of Gilgamesh*, and the trail only runs cold there because the archaeology of the written word does. It's not a question of colonising the past and extending modernism back through the centuries. Rather, it is to merely detect what's already there when we look back.

Let's begin with the more cursory signs that an authoritative date of origin cannot be established; we find these most obviously in the great disruptors of early twentieth century culture, the progenitors of the new primitivism. When the colonialists sent back plunder from the lands and peoples they'd invaded and subjugated, they did so to create a sort of imperial *wunderkammer*, a cabinet of curiosities gathered from the farthest reaches of their territories. The exotic and unrefined nature of the artefacts would prove, by contrast, the superiority of civilisation. They made, however, a costly mistake displaying their thefts. The artists were watching, many of them godless cosmopolitans, immigrants and bohemians. Whilst their discoveries were only in the sense of Columbus discovering the Americas, they nonetheless had a profound effect on the course of modern culture, challenging the orthodoxies and establishments of art. When you view Munch's *The Scream*, you are seeing a work inspired, not just by the artist's breakdown ('I stood there trembling with anxiety—and I sensed an infinite shriek passing through nature') but by the silent cadaverous shriek of a Peruvian mummy he'd viewed in the Louvre. The very same skeleton appeared as a harbinger of death in *Where Do We Come From? What Are We? Where Are We Going?* by Paul Gauguin, another anxiety-riven edge of suicide masterpiece. Similarly, Picasso's radical *Les Demoiselles d'Avignon* was partially based on African and Oceanic tribal masks (the artist had picked up masks (re)stolen from the Louvre on the black-market), as were early disconcertingly 'new' Giacometti sculptures such as *Statue of a Deceased Woman* and *Invisible Object*. When critics railed against the 'atonality' of Stravinsky's *Rite of Spring*—Debussy stormed out at the 'improper use of a bassoon'—they were simply admitting their ignorance or distaste of musical modes and scales beyond the Western post-Diatonic (most of the world's music in effect). To make a great leap forwards, sometimes you have to take a few steps back, or look in another direction.

This reinvention through appropriation is not new or problematic to anyone but the territorial and the delusional. No artist is an island, culture is an echo-chamber, and these influences were no doubt influenced in turn. It's possible to decipher the triskele spirals of Ancient Celtic stonework in the gilded swirls of Klimt for example. Joyce famously used Homer's *Odyssey* as the blueprint for a day in the life of a cuckolded Jewish Dubliner in *Ulysses*. In doing so, he rendered the everyday epic and the epic everyday. Less well-known is Musil's adaptation of the Ancient Egyptian Isis and Osiris myth for the final book of *The Man Without Qualities*. Rilke, Cocteau, Trakl and Apollinaire all turned to Orpheus. As we now see the earlier works through the prism of that which they inspired (Virgil through Dante for instance), there is considerable truth to Borges' bold claim that 'a great writer creates his 'predecessors.'

Everything is fragmented, even the self. No one believes in anything. We are atomised. All is transitory and in flux. 'My souls (characters) are conglomerations of past and present stages of civilization,' Strindberg claimed, 'bits from books and newspapers, pieces of human beings, rags and tatters of fine clothing, patched together like the human soul.' We are those characters. To Herbert Read, modernism was 'not so much a revolution, which implies a turning over, even a turning back, but rather a break-up, a devolution, some would say a dissolution. Its character is catastrophic.' We are alone in facing this catastrophe. 'To be modern,'

Declan Kiberd has claimed, 'is to experience perpetual disintegration and renewal and yet somehow to make a home in that disorder.' This may well all be true. What is omitted is that life and certainly art have always been like this. Classicism, with its Doric columns and pentameters, was after all an invention. What makes disorder appear a recent development is that we've lost the suspension of disbelief to have faith in the illusion, or aspiration, of order. Just as we are credulous enough to assume that the Ancient Greeks believed in the gods and myths they invented, so too do we ignore the upheavals, uncertainties, destructions and the ever changing aspects to life then. The aesthetic attempts at symmetry and unity have partially survived in archaeology; the chaos they were created from and to replace is often forgotten. Cybernetics, chaos theory, evolution, all of these phenomena existed then.

In *The Mind of Modernism*, James McFarlane was wise enough to see that our view of what is ancient and what is modern was warped through the prism of solipsism, 'Were this all that is characteristic of modernism—a viper's tangle in which yes and no, life and death, man and woman [...] there would be little real novelty. The notion of the reconciliation of opposites is in itself at least as old as Heraclitus.' The ability to look two ways at once, that seemingly modern trait, is indeed millennia-old. In Ancient Rome, they even had the two-faced god Janus embodying this, a god that was also fittingly the god of entrances and perpetually-occurring beginnings. The ability to abandon either/or and embrace cognitive dissonance is there in Eubulides' line 'I am lying' or 'This statement is false,' a proto-Schrödinger's Cat paradox that is simultaneously true and untrue. Ezra Pound was mischievously aware of the possibilities of something being 'both/and' when he borrowed his call-to-arms 'Make it new' from an inscription on a Chinese Emperor's washbasin.

Literary 'truth' and Reason have always had the element of wishful thinking, one reinforced by the Enlightenment, which for all its admirable free enquiry was a curious attempt to regain our collective innocence. The questioning of Reason, its deconstruction from various angles, goes way back beyond Derrida, Nietzsche or Hegel and Kant's squabbles. Before he drank himself to death, the Sceptic philosopher Arcesilaus asserted that we could be certain of nothing, even, paradoxically, our own ignorance. Anaxagoras believed that everything was once fragmented, interspersed and endlessly interconnected and that it was the mind that segregated things and gave the appearance of order. We are moving still, in the dim light, in that direction.

In *Hermotimus, or the Rival Philosophies*, Lucian assessed the difficulty of finding something to cling to, 'The truth is hidden from us. Even if a mere piece of luck brings us straight to it, we shall have no grounded conviction of our success; there are so many similar objects, all claiming to be the real thing.' The untrustworthy nature of art and consciousness is brilliantly displayed in his *True Story*. A work of science fiction before there was a clearly-defined field of science, it contains telescopes, aliens, robots, space travel and inter-planetary warfare. In an introductory statement, he captures the essence of fiction, 'I now make the only true statement you are to expect—that I am a liar... My subject is what I have neither seen, experienced, nor been told, what neither exists nor could conceivably do so. I humbly solicit my readers' incredulity.' This is also underlined in *On Unbelievable Tales* by Palaephatus, which examines the origin of contemporaneous myths, deeds that had been metaphorical but were taken as literal—pirates ships mistaken for sea beasts, men on horseback becoming centaurs, miners subterranean creatures. The passage of time and the effect of Chinese whispers might make such tales seem plausible when they are not Palaephatus warned. In believing that the Ancients believed unquestioning in myths, we are being considerably more naive than they were. We may think we are uniquely sophisticated with a cynical edge compared to the gullible troglodytes who came before us, but we grossly underestimate them and overestimate ourselves. And as they taught, hubris will eventually meet nemesis. They were after all cynical enough to call the Black Sea, notorious place of storms and shipwrecks *Euxine* ('the hospitable') and their paradise Elysium originating from *enelysios* meaning 'struck by lightning.'

The idea that objectivity is inherently compromised and set on shifting sands of perception, context and even semantics, and the 'modern' anxiety that arouses, is discussed at length by Hermias,

> 'Some say the soul is fire...some say it is the mind; and some say it is motion...Why must we term these things? They seem to me, to be a prodigy, or folly, or madness, or rebellion, or all these together...I confess I am harassed by the ebbing and flowing of the subject.

> At one time I am immortal and rejoice; at another time again I become mortal and weep. Anew I am dissolved into atoms: I become water, and I become air: I become fire, and then after a little, neither air, nor fire: he makes me a beast, he makes me a fish…The beginning of all things is mind, and this is the cause and regulator of all things, and gives arrangement to things unarranged, and motion to things unmoved, and distinction to things mixed, and order to things disordered.'

Beset by an inability to grasp any form of certainty, or rather suffering from the vertigo of modernity, Hermias concludes, 'all worldly knowledge is madness from God.'

The Cynics formed a sturdier line in the face of the same problem. Bion of Borysthenes resolutely attacked everything, from the top down, 'How stupid it was for the king to tear out his hair in grief, as if baldness were a cure for sorrow.' Less antagonistic, Pyrrhon of Elis accepted that nothing can be definitively known and noted the abandonment of concern resulted in *ataraxia* ('freedom from worry'). The two approaches may have their flaws (Bion's could result in a shortened lifespan, Pyrrhon's in a self-satisfied stupor) but both resemble modern approaches to intractable political problems; the permanent revolution (or rather the play of revolution) of satire and the blissful ignorance of hedonism and quasi-Buddhism. Both are a form of stepping outside.

What brings about the requisite angst is worth looking at. There are innumerable social, economic, political and psychological factors (from the inequities of capitalism to the fault-lines of childhood) but one thing is clear: every generation is re-enacting the Great Disillusionment. For some, there is a cataclysmic event, which speeds up and amplifies the process immensely (the First World War, the Holocaust and so on). Occasionally, a much smaller event acts as a catalyst or a spotlight for a disenchantment that would eventually come to pass regardless. It acts as a metaphor and outlet for underlying and building tensions. The events have a power because they cut through omnipresent and perhaps necessary societal denial about the nature of who and what we are as creatures. It happened in Rome with the loss of three entire legions (20,000 men) in the Teutoburg Forest, their skulls found years later nailed to the trees. It happened in Victorian England with the loss of *HMS Terror* and *HMS Erebus* and news of their cannibalised crew, wandering mad in the Arctic wastes. Chivalry is stillborn, good and evil much more intertwined than we wish. The realisation happens still periodically in real life, and always will, not least in the cracked mirror of art—the epiphanies that litter the works of Joyce, Woolf, Grosz, Chaucer, Dostoyevsky, Camus, Plath and Céline—to name just a few of what must constitute every real writer and artist in effect. We are constantly undergoing The Fall because we constantly insist on believing in innocence and in things being as we would wish rather than as they really are.

The ability of art to jolt us out of complacency is an archaic technique in relatively-new clothes. When Bertolt Brecht spoke of his estrangement technique (*Verfremdungseffekt*) in theatre, picked up from Shklovsky and pre-empting

Derrida's *différance*, it seemed that he was doing something startlingly fresh. The audience might be awakened from their slumber, able to consider the political and social ramifications of the play, their own levels of culpability and privilege (or lack of) rather than being seduced or lulled into acquiescence by what he scornfully called, 'culinary theatre.' Was this fundamentally different from the role of the Greek chorus?—a question tacitly acknowledged by Brecht who labelled his style of theatre *nicht Aristotelisches* (non-Aristotelian). Homer had anticipated this in the *Odyssey* with the Land of the Lotus-eaters, where Odysseus' crew feast and lose all thoughts of returning home. Art could be a narcotic and, worst of all, an opiate. It would take a focused mind like Odysseus' or Brecht's for that matter, and another form of art to force us back onboard the ship.

When the event in question is so monumentally harrowing, how can any response be adequate? There's an understandable mute paralysis to Theodor Adorno's line 'After Auschwitz, there can be no poetry' to which Paul Celan gave an unintended response with 'Death Fugue,' a haunting bewildering poem that barely seems like any other. Having endured years of electroshock therapy, incarcerated during the Occupation, Antonin Artaud responded with primal noise. Our wielding of language, with its justifications and deceptions, had led us to the gas-chambers. Artaud abandoned it for what he called 'a vortex,' his Theatre of Cruelty consisting of spasmodic shrieks and contortions with the representational aspect of art obliterated. It was pure uncomfortable experience but one with roots in Balinese dance and the rites of Dionysus, the *mainomenoas*—'the raving god.' It was perhaps an attempt at accusation or exorcism, to start again or finish, as if we ever could.

Though Artaud could attempt to escape language, it is not possible to escape the tyranny of context. When the dadaists revolted against the patriotic anthems and jingoism that brought Europe to self-immolation, they did so partially through nonsense language. Hugo Ball was not just conjuring up some new international language of gibberish or calling into question what language is and means with his poem 'Karawane' ('jolifanto bambla o falli bambla / großiga m'pfa habla horem'), he was, like Artaud, performing the ancient art of glossolalia or speaking in tongues. Just as the apostles had responded to the trauma of their messiah being executed with tall-tales of resurrection and then a chorus of possessed supernatural utterings, so too the dadaists responded to the trauma of a continent at war with itself with babble. The dadaists knew that nothing means nothing. Associations inevitably spiral off as synapses fire. Even the name *dada*, picked for its meaninglessness, is said to originate from the French for 'hobbyhorse,' the Romanian for 'yes, yes,' or paternal baby-talk. It does not matter whether it has a definitive meaning or even if such a thing is possible; it is what we perceive it to be. Similarly for the apostles, it is not what the holy spirit might be saying with our tongues as its vessel, it is what we want to hear that matters.

God, if such a thing were any less ephemeral or man-made than Reason, can appear in other manifestations. We might see the use of a device like Deus ex machina, when a deity is mechanically lowered in from the rafters or appears in

a puff of smoke from a trapdoor to resolve some intractable plot dead-end, as a dusty old device unworthy of a decent playwright. This was a common view in Ancient Greece with Euripides continually castigated for his fondness for the cop-out; most scathingly by Aristophanes who unceremoniously swings the playwright as Perseus in on his own device in *Thesmophoriazusae*. A modern writer would never dare employ such a ham-fisted resolution unless we consider the ingenuity of our microscopic saviours, the bacteria in *The War of the Worlds* or of Raymond Chandler's secular adaptation, 'When in doubt, have a man come through a door with a gun in his hand.'

The layers of narrative and perception that are characteristic of modernist and postmodernist writing, the irreverent games, contradictions and unreliable narration were all at play aeons ago; *meta*, after all, is an Ancient Greek word. Incidences of what we might term conceptual or experimental fiction abound in age-old tales. Tales exist within tales in Heliodorus' *Ethiopian Story* and *Deipnosophistae* by Athenaeus, the latter being employed to subtly mock its gastronomic cast and the prevailing thoughts of the day. In Apuleius' *The Golden Ass*, there are shifting and unreliable narrators, picaresque encounters, twists and double twists. The concept of mimesis finds expression in Plato or rather Socrates' symbolic three beds—the idea of a bed (conceived by God), the physicality of a bed (made by a carpenter) and the artistic rendering of a bed. Alongside Socrates' allegory of the Cave, the idea acts as an integral precursor to Descartes, Wittgenstein, the Situationist spectacle, Magritte's *The Treachery of Images* (*'Ceci n'est pas une pipe'*) and endlessly multiplying schools of thought that all is not as it seems and there is something behind everything. Before he and a sidekick ran off laughing into the mountains, the Chinese poet Han Shan etched his verse as graffiti onto bamboo, cliff-faces, rocks which the governor of the area had written down for posterity. It was poetry, conceptual art and performance, the breakdown of the barrier between form and content, and possibly none of the above in its creator's mind.

If we take playful and occasionally lacerating self-reference to be modern then Ovid is a modern writer. He flaunts a level of wry knowing, irony and a willingness to let the reader in on it all (as Plautus does with his deceptions) that defy any surface reading of his *Amores* (The Loves), *Ars Amatoria* (The Art of Love) and *Epistulae Heroidum* (Letters of Heroines). This flirting with meta ('what harm will a letter do?') would prove costly for Ovid who was banished from Rome by the Emperor for, in his own words, 'a song and a mistake'. 'My books have hurt no one but myself / the author's own life was ruined by his 'Art,"' he continues, somewhat disingenuously, given his curse sequence *Ibis* is one of the most exquisitely bile-soaked screeds committed to text (even if its revenge, like Dante's *Inferno* is a description of sullen impotence),

> 'Let earth deny its fruits to you, the rivers their waves, let the winds and the breezes deny you their breath. Let there be no heat to the sun, for you, no light for you from the moon, let all the bright stars forsake your eyes.'

Written in his Black Sea exile, Ovid's *Tristia* (Sorrows) have proved immensely influential to writers since, especially those forced into exile; whether external (Dante), internal (Osip Mandelstam borrowed the title for his second post-Revolution book) or a migration by choice (Ovid was crucial to Joyce's conception of Stephen Dedalus in *Portrait* and *Ulysses*). Applying a multiplicity of views to the text as well as the self, the opening lines of the book address the book itself, 'Little book, go without me—I don't begrudge it—to the city / Ah, alas, that your master's not allowed to go!' This is echoed at the end of Ovid's *Thebaid*, when he ponders artistic immortality, speaking not just to his book but to the not yet born, 'Wilt thou endure in the time to come, O my Thebaid, for twelve years object of my wakeful toil, wilt thou survive thy master and be read? [...] O live, I pray!'

Blamed by Tom Stoppard for the invention of love as we know it, Propertius demonstrates a multi-faceted view of the subject and the legacy it leaves. 'It is a shame,' he writes in verse to a Muse (with the logic of Eubulides Paradox) 'that my verse has made you famous.' In contrast to the naive courtly love we might expect, he shows it can be a wretched thing,

> 'Even now, the gods are against me… yet I didn't dare disturb my mistress' quiet, fearing the outbursts of her expert cruelty. Poor boy, you're rushing into a hellhole!'

He addresses friends, naysayers, distracting adventurers and enemies and, in all the correspondence, love is a blissful curse, 'I saw you, Gallus, dying, wrapped / in her arms, engaged in a long, languorous dialogue! ... He will remain happy with one girl /who will be never free, never thoughtless.'

Acute self-awareness informs commendably self-deprecating verse in Horace's *Satires*,

> 'You write so little, Horace, you barely trouble The copyist four times a year, always unravelling The web you've woven, angered with yourself because, Despite lots of wine and sleep, nothing's done to speak of.'

Archilochus goes further with sexually explicit, gleefully-cowardly and above all mercilessly-honest writing that would do Henry Miller proud centuries later. 'One of the Saiôn in Thrace now delights in the shield I discarded / Unwillingly near a bush, for it was perfectly good, / But at least I got myself safely out. Why should I care for that shield? / Let it go. Some other time I'll find another no worse.' This is a man who sees through it all and bravely admits so, who has come to the conclusion that honour be damned or at least that there is a honour in dishonour. What it recalls is not some hoary old text but the eternal struggle between political commitment and personal happiness, a question explored by George Orwell in his essay on reading and meeting Miller *Inside the Whale*. Despite many centuries separating them, Archilochus and Henry Miller are contemporaries.

If a delight in degradation and despair can equally bridge the millennia then Aristophanes and Samuel Beckett are comrades-in-arms. Reading the words of the chorus in *The Birds*, you get the sense of Beckett's eloquent wallowing in the mire particularly in novels like *Watt*, 'Ye Children of Man! whose life is a span, / Protracted with sorrow from day to day, / Naked and featherless, feeble and querulous, / Sickly, calamitous creatures of clay! ... Weak mortals, chained to the earth, creatures of clay as frail as the foliage of the woods, you unfortunate race, whose life is but darkness, as unreal as a shadow, the illusion of a dream.' Aristophanes would also equip modern writers with the ability to satirise in the best way; from oblique, unexpected and invulnerable angles. The fantastical settings and occurrences of his writing and the scathing truths about real human frailty and corruption therein find different but unmistakable incarnations in the writings of Jonathan Swift, Bulgakov, Gogol, the surrealists, the Theatre of the Absurd, Brecht, Václav Havel, Andrey Kurkov, the animation of Jan Svankmajer and so on. 'Man is least himself,' wrote Oscar Wilde, 'when he talks in his own person. Give him a mask, and he will tell you the truth.' The same goes for cloud cities, giants, depressed penguins, cats that walk upright, noses that have lives of their own. Unable to truly 'make it new' or ,'make it true,' we can at least, to paraphrase Shklovsky, 'make it strange.'

Sometimes the magic described seeped into the text itself. In medieval times, the writings of Virgil were seen by some as possessing supernatural properties in terms of predicting the future, what is known as bibliomancy. The *Sortes Virgilianae*

(Virgilian Lottery) involved delving into the *Aeneid* and extracting random lines which would then be interpreted for divinatory clues. There was in fact a long tradition of this, incorporating texts by Ovid and Homer as well as the *I Ching* and the holy books of all the major religions. Words had power and not just of the ordinary time-travelling, talking to the dead, bridging of consciousness kinds. We might dismiss such acts as the acts of folly and desperation by barely-literate superstitious 'dark age' denizens but the practise has had durability as an experimental technique. Philip K. Dick has the characters in his *The Man in the High Castle* use the method, one which he in turn used when plotting the novel. The surrealists employed various games of chance in their creative processes most famously in *cadavre exquis* but also bulletism, frottage, cubomania, *éclaboussure*, *coulage* and entopic graphomania. Chance rather than god or magic was the supposed guiding hand though it was still presumed to have a ghostly sentient element. To B.S. Johnson, the chance assemblage of his 'book in a box,' *The Unfortunates*, was a preferable conclusion, or lack of, than anything he could have chosen himself. From the dadaist Tristan Tzara and the surrealist idea of 'latent news,' William Burroughs and Brion Gysin cribbed their cut-up method, about which Burroughs claimed, 'When you cut into the present the future leaks out.' Superstitions are ideas, however malformed, and ideas do not die.

It is worth reminding ourselves that concepts such as Lacan's gaze and *objet petit a* or Freud's id and ego are ageless phenomena, which they identified rather than invented. It is we who link them to their precedents and antecedents. It's entirely possible to argue that Freud's talking or writing cure found expression centuries ago in the practise of Catharsis, as discussed in Aristotle's *Poetics*. Or that the subconscious found manifestation in the mythic underworld; psyche coming from the Greek spirit of the dead. We might concede that psychogeography had a past life as the ancient Irish *Dindsenchas* ('lore of places') tradition or the Aboriginal Songlines or Pausanias' *Descriptions of Greece* where place is wedded with myth and legend. We can acknowledge that Nietzsche was turning Lucian's *Kataplous* (Downward Journey) on its head to create his *übermensch*, ignoring the valuable lesson therein on the dangers of hubris. In a similar sense, the gnostics believed the human body to be venal and inferior and transcendence was the logical next step pre-empting not only Nietzsche but trans-humanist philosophers like Max More and Nick Bostrom. We have been *Human, All Too Human* since we first flopped onto dry land.

We might recognise that the anti-hero was born not in noir or *Paradise Lost* but much further back: Cú Chulainn with his chariot festooned with human heads, Achilles dragging Hector's body around Troy or Odysseus slaughtering Penelope's suitors. We might also recognise that this challenge to our sentimentalised Manichean conceptions of good and evil is a necessary one. We can recognise Werner Herzog's 'ecstatic truth' in Longinus' treatise *On the Sublime* and the flashbacks of Ford Maddox Ford's *The Good Soldier* in *The Ramayana*. We can detect the voices of the Cynics in Tristan Tzara's claim that 'Dada is useless, like everything else in life' and Wilde's and Gautier's 'All art is quite useless,' a crucial ingredient in the development of 'Art for art's sake.' Aeschylus and Dickens were masters of the reversal of fortune (*peripeteiai*). In the *Satires* of Horace we find the embryonic Pylon Poets, Mayakovsky and Brecht. Persius' words 'All Romans have asses ears' is uttered into a hole in the ground echoing Julia's words to Winston Smith 'I LOVE YOU' placed into the memory-hole in *1984*. Even the anti-tradition of the Futurists, urging the flooding and incineration of museums, finds a place in the long tradition of iconoclasm.

Consider Philip Larkin's pitch black words in 'This Be The Verse,' often celebrated as introducing a refreshing scorn into post-Romantic poetry,

> 'Man hands on misery to man.
>   It deepens like a coastal shelf.
> Get out as early as you can,
>   And don't have any kids yourself.'

Now compare them to Theognis' lines from the sixth century BC,

> 'Best of all for mortal beings is never to have been born at all
> Nor ever to have set eyes on the bright light of the sun
> But, since he is born, a man should make utmost haste through the gates of Death
> And then repose, the earth piled into a mound round himself.'

It's possible to chart currents through themes, methods, subjects and subgenres linking vanished civilisations with ours. Achilles' heel is Chekhov's gun in a sense: one must receive an arrow as the other must be fired, instilling a sense of narrative tension in their respective stories. The stream of consciousness technique used by Joyce and Woolf, pioneered by Édouard Dujardin and Knut Hamsun has existed as the *Citta-samtana* ('stream of the mind') in Buddhist literature for hundreds of years. The use of the seriocomic method *spoudaiogeloion* (according to Horace 'what forbids one to tell the truth while laughing') forms the basis of much comic but piercing writing from the likes of Flann O'Brien, Kurt Vonnegut and Gunter Grass where laughter is a Trojan Horse and tragedy all the more poignant in juxtaposition. The mix of verse and prose (*prosimetrum*) in Nabokov's *Pale Fire* finds an ancestor in Basho's *The Narrow Road to the Deep North*, *The Madness of King Sweeney*, the *Mahabharata* and Petronius' *Satyricon*. Beloved of noir (Dashiell Hammett) and literary fiction (Bolaño's *2666*, Durrell's *The Alexandria Quartet*, Faulkner's *Light in August*), the *in medias res* technique, where the story begins in the middle and flicks backwards and forwards, was evident in Odysseus' earliest appearance in *The Odyssey* trapped with Calypso on the island of Ogygia. Similarly, the reverse chronology that we might see as modern and experimental in Martin Amis' *Times Arrow* (inspired by a scene in which the war appears to wind backwards in Vonnegut's *Slaughterhouse-Five*) appeared in Virgil's *Aeniad* and *One Thousand and One Nights*. When Huxley wrote of his experiences with LSD, or Burroughs of Yage, they were doing so in the wisdom through debauchery tradition of the

Greek Symposium, the Native American sweathouse and Li Bai and the Eight Immortals of the Wine Cup. When Eliot shored the fragments against his ruin, he was doing little that Confucius, Sei Shonagon, Sallust and Heraclitus did not do before him. All literature is gathered fragments and, as Sappho could testify, time makes fragments of all literature eventually.

Often there can be a cautionary lesson to glean from the links between the modern and the ancient. In Bakhtin's *Rabelais and His World*, the theorist introduces his concept of the 'carnivalesque' his observance of how festivals act as a temporary suspension of social boundaries and class. Everyone can socialise together for as long as the carnival lasts and all is permitted. This was an established practice during the Greek Saturnalia of which Horace wrote, addressing a slave, 'Come on, then, use the freedom / December allows, since our ancestors wished it: speak!' It is tempting to view such times as a social leveller, a glimpse of what after the revolution might look like. Yet the time was necessary to act as a pressure release for social tensions. It was meant to prevent revolution and sustain oppression for the rest of the year. The slave may be able to say what he or she likes to the master during the carnival but they will see many less festivals during their shortened life-span.

Class distinctions found their way also into the separation of high and low art. Stories like *The Ephesian Tale of Anthia and Habrocomes* by Xenophon were as castigated as soap operas, Hollywood movies or pulp. The denigration had much to do with a priestly cultural caste establishing itself as the arbiters of taste and monopolisers of knowledge, as with certain parts of academia and the commentariat today. Despite acting as crucial reservoirs of stories, travelling rhapsodists and sophists were demonised for existing without the permission of these culture-bearers and also because of the fear their words might have real power (it was said effective satire in Ireland could raise boils on the skin of its targets). The establishment of court jesters were not simply to preserve objective truth for monarchs in courts filled with sycophants; they were also to neutralise satire from outside. We might think we are immune to such snobbish and intransigent views until we recall how the Beat Generation were treated by the literary establishment of their day or more recently the reaction to James Kelman's Booker win.

The revelation that the lives of ordinary working people were worthy of writing literature was likewise made long ago; Alciphron raised it to rhetorical heights and the mix of high art and low life in *The Waste Land* was evident in the parodies, curses, recipes and elegies of *Appendix Vergiliana* with its song of the seductress barmaid Syrisca and its evicted nameless farmer calling down floods and fires upon his landlord. The modernist focus on the body and the inferred abolition (or at least exploration) of shame, which emerged in Joyce, Lawrence, and Beckett (Bakhtin's 'grotesque body' theory), has its roots not just in licentious literature like Byron or the bawdy moments of Chaucer but further back in Petronius' *Satyricon* (as resurrected by Fellini) and Aristophanes' *The Knights*. More succinctly, there is the unearthed graffiti of Pompeii, preserved by pyroclastic flow, where poetry and messages to the gods are written alongside messages such as 'Theophilus, don't perform oral sex on girls against the city wall like a dog' and 'Phileros is a eunuch!'

Less obvious or exalted modern mediums were rehearsed in the far-flung past. The still-compelling wisdom of Marcus Aurelius' *Meditations* and Seneca's *On the Transience of Life* could be seen as prototype self-help tracts, if we were to degrade such masterpieces by association. Blues music is an often-overlooked modern idiom and it's worth remembering the likes of Blind Boy Fuller were contemporaries of Joyce and co. Many of the lyrics of blues standards are as magic realist ('St James Infirmary' for example), violent ('A to Z Blues') and sexually explicit ('Shave 'em Dry') as the most edgy contemporary novel. Yet the blues was not strictly new, employing not just the general laments of old (the Gaelic 'songs of sorrow' *Goltraighe*) but specific forms like the Augustan Paraclausithyron where a suitor lusts for their muse behind a door or the 'Gambler's Lament' of the Hindu Rigveda in which an addict curses the magnetism of the dice that brought him to ruin and the loss of family and friends.

Even the rap battle of the present has precursors in bucolic amoebaean poetry duels. Shepherds would face-off verbally, with the first to repeat or contradict an earlier statement losing. In Theocritus' *Fifth Idyll*, Lacon and Comatas abuse each other in glorious terms, 'you dare look me in the face, I that had the teaching of you when you were but a child...Those buckgoat-pelts of thine smell e'en ranker than thou... Most excellent blockhead, all I say is true, I'm no braggart... Somebody's waxing wild; see you not what is plain? / Go pluck him squills from an old wife's grave to cool his heated brain.' Insults would often revolve around who received better fortune from the gods as well as physical, sexual and shepherding prowess. A transitional figure between the throw-downs of then and now is the scientist and writer Paracelsus whose insults and boasts rival the dexterity and megalomania of hip-hop braggadocio, 'You are not learned or experienced enough to refute even a word of mine... Let me tell you this: every little hair on my neck knows more than you and all your scribes, and my shoe buckles are more learned than your Galen and Avicenna, and my beard has more experience than all your high colleges.'

Given that modernism is an amorphous entity and something of a retrospective invention, it's useful to look at the unlikely power of ancient writing over individual modern writers. Whilst the influence of Apuleius' *The Golden Ass* on pioneering conceptual fiction like *Don Quixote*, *Candide* and *Tristram Shandy*, it was also a crucial influence on Franz Kafka. The metamorphosis in the earlier work had an obvious parallel, though the direct source of Gregor Samsa was Kafka's father's use of the insult *Ungeziefer* ('bug') to describe his son. Less obvious was the role book three of *The Golden Ass* would have on the writer, particularly his book *The Trial*. In one, Lucius awakes and is promptly arrested. In the other, Josef K. undergoes the same. Lucius escapes through metamorphosis; Gregor Samsa meets his end through it. The difference is pessimism; for Apuleius, this is all comedy, for Kafka tragedy, or perhaps comedy at his expense (and ours) and for the benefit of someone or something unseen.

The Satyricon also casts a long shadow, partially on F. Scott Fitzgerald's *The Great Gatsby*. The earlier tale of nouveau riche libertinage, the grotesqueries of wealth and the vapidity of status had such an effect on Fitzgerald's work that he came close to naming the novel *Trimalchio in West Egg* (or *Trimalchio* or *Gold-Hatted Gatsby*) after one of its characters. If we take the lavish but haunted Gatsby as Trimalchio reincarnated it throws Fitzgerald's book into a fascinating different light. Petronius' character throws characteristically extravagant parties with live birds inside suckling pigs and indulges himself by rehearsing his own sumptuous funeral. His guests are trapped and have to escape from the festivities. If Gatsby is as much an example of the emptiness of the American Dream and the impossibility of striving for the impossible as *Moby Dick* is, then Gatsby's world is as much a prison for he and his guests as Trimalchio's party. Is it a failure or an attempt to escape that defines the last trace of the Satryicon left in Fitzgerald's novel? 'It was when curiosity about Gatsby was at its highest that the lights in his house failed to go on one Saturday night—and, as obscurely as it began, his career as Trimalchio was over.'

Unfurling the allusions in the work of James Joyce would take a labyrinthine library but one identifiable strand linking him to the past is his feminism. Molly Bloom's stream of consciousness monologue in *Ulysses* and the two washerwomen of *Finnegans Wake* recall Theocritus' *Idyll #15* in which the rambling apparently throwaway gossip hides profound truths ('Trying took Troy'). There are wise cursory glances towards men ('my lunatic') but also a subversive depiction of freedom, community and covert power ('My dear, women know everything') below the male radar and before, and despite, fading away.

When Kant was searching for a motto for the Enlightenment, against the tyranny of ignorance and its profiteers, he found it in Horace's epistles 'Sapere aude'—'Dare to know.' Those scientists furtively discovering the world of atoms could take solace in the fact that Democritus had prophesied atomic theory around 400 BC. In his book *The Swerve: How the World Became Modern*, Stephen Greenblatt goes so as far as to say the Renaissance and Enlightenment were sparked by the saving (by the humanist Poggio Bracciolini) and rereading of a single copy of Lucretius' *On the Nature of Things*, which had been mouldering away in a German monastery. Modernity itself owes everything to the rediscovery of ancient Greek texts and continuation of their explorations after the 'Dark Ages' of theocracy.

The idea that nothing is completely new and history is helical may seem a reactionary one but that would be a superficial reading. Nothing is new and yet everything is new to someone. If we accept the solipsism that we only ever exist in the present then modernism and ancient culture only exist now. 'There is no was,' as Faulkner pointed out. The patron saint of writers and the one who most understood the magic of books in transcending time, mortality and authorship, Jorge Luis Borges was attributed as saying, 'I am not sure that I exist. I am all the writers that I have read, all the people that I have met, all the women that I have loved; all the cities that I have visited, all my ancestors.' Elsewhere, in *A Note on (toward) Bernard Shaw*, he wrote 'A book is more than a verbal structure or series of verbal structures; it is the dialogue it establishes with its reader and the intonation it imposes upon his voice and the changing and durable images it leaves in his memory. A book is not an isolated being: it is a relationship, an axis of innumerable relationships.' Some might feel profoundly dispirited at the inter-connectedness of things and the weight of history, burdens that challenge our infantile attraction to originality and authenticity. If we have courage, they have however the power to liberate us. William Gibson famously stated, 'The future is already here—it's just not very evenly distributed.' Many forget this has *always* been the case. When we look back, we can discover the present and the future hidden in the past, just as much as we can recreate it. Despite what we might initially think, this is a radical idea. There is no lost utopia centuries ago, no Garden of Eden or and no Fall from grace. There is only the most monumental scrapyard with innumerable paths through it. All history is there and it's ours for the taking, along with the present and future, if we can only begin to make the connections.

Inverted Yearning
Julie Reverb

Her dad's death is neatly assuaged in a late-night murmuring era. It's not yet complete, but there are crying walks, alone. He'd seen Roy Orbison once, at Caesars Palace. Cry-i-i-i-ing over you.

She smokes and watches and thinks on the family business. What will happen to them. The picture has bruised edges she cannot touch, not even with her ring finger. The rabbits aren't moving and mum is stalling her words. They trail off in their unthinking, smoky letters across a dithering sky. Her dressing-gown belt wilts to the floor, a sigh across domestic tundra. Mum broods in her tea-making. Pouring glides into tepid stirring then forgetting. Where are the biscuits—did she leave them in the car? Did she buy any? They sit apart while the dog concedes into a quarter circle. Deciding against life, dreaming the end. Light lays a sickly wash on the grass; legs buckle on dew. Neighbours wash their cars; grey water curls slowly to their doors in indifferent dousing. Her bare feet buoyed by wet grit. She's overstretched yet cannot sleep. The rooms are dazed; their shadows console but are strained, flinching from hardness and insult. They give up at night, shrinking into quiet and knowing. A nodding and impotent slinking on the landing. A sloughing of tender pride from bone. I told you so. The net curtains bristle and doubt themselves in the draft. Moths move above a piss in the dark. Someone has left the room. A sloppy grin at a pale ceiling. Lucy, let down your hair.

At my age you won't want a green banana.

Lucy sits facing Billy, tossing spaghetti. She rubs it up against itself, in circles of hell and denial, climbing up walls and collapsing off steel. She is not hungry, not going anywhere, so she morbidly waits, making murder at the table. She is aware of uncertainty as a bathing halo—her chair against tile, her future, whether the waiter will glance at Billy miming writing in the air. She eyes the odds of her roller-skating dreams, versus the business of brusque labial display. She does not want to be pinned, pressed among promised hurts that fall in sequence. She sees pain as stained glass, paused glinting pitfalls that confront. There's only so much inverted yearning you can take. The stuff in between just disgusts. She's pleased they didn't go easy on the garlic: the handshake will taunt the truth.

The truth about sitting on a see-saw. How long have you got?

He has been counting his blinks until now, exalting in newer seeing and the happiness that surely waits for him this time. It is his for once, his claim to a throne—a bicycle made for two—and it cannot be clawed or refunded. It is not made of piled dirt, nor deserted on a causeway. His exiled years have ended; this is his last push into glossy terminal moraine. No more drunken mornings waiting for the postman to pass his window, or being chased around tables with snapped pool cues. No more Alzheimered desire and startled hardness, no gumminess looking for lost words. He wonders will his stools be firmer now; he won't have to hide or stoop or smudge himself, folding paper like confessions. The greatest want rests in his lap. He feels casually death-proof, sitting straight among the romancing and birthdaying units stacked across tile. He toys with suggesting dessert; he has leached the Ouroboros that choked shame into his face since youth.

'Sorry?' says Lucy.

He sees himself as he was once: helpless, the youngest, bundled knees in the middle as wheels underneath churn soil. A cramped dirge across barrenness in a Vauxhall hatchback, all child-locks and muted morning breath. The driver's hand a benign clamp on the gear-stick, his gold ring glinting in the rueful turning toward morning. His pampas grass eyebrow in rear-view mirror and eye locked on the cloying now. Sand-headed men smother their yawns from must and something once living in the glove-box. Pigeons pick bones outside. Billy wants to say something, to call it off with a ghost-limbed group hug. His belly rumbles into rain-pocked sides of dampness seeping out over a baby-seat. A hint of piss and a bloating inevitability. Her mute, snowy face in his wallet spoons the queen's. She says nothing and reveals less. Weighty, tired squints imbricate on the rubbish outside, on the gulls and spoils. 'The cattle are lowing Billy. The buck stopped a while back,' Mad Sinbad says. He turns the radio dial. Billy can still hear the *'there there'* of Cromarty and Dogger, the waves knocking against a little boat somewhere out on the North Sea. To be a man of lulls and escapes and a radio career. Slippers gently placed the right way under the bed. Keys in a not so obvious place. A nicely full stomach and kind waking to days spread out like a picnic blanket. Careful folding and a hand held in the hospital. Quiet structure shared. Tears grace-noted, smoothed with soft fingers. The gentleness you bring to dying skin. I looked at her with big slabs of eye, big ol' china plates; I was drinking her in as I knew it would be the last time. She sensed something—splitting or tightening—and smiled more keenly, maybe she thought I was drunk or plain happy, for real and not bought this time. Us sinking ships together, toe-dippers at the brink. Me losing my footing, a trip over a rabbit hole, hobbling agony of my heart spooked on a missed stair. It is all too late, his was never the right horse, he was too busy fumbling during the safety demo, a last-minute Houdini understudy against a slow-clapping tide.

'I never understood a thing he said—sausage-meat snipped with intakes of breath. It was years before I worked out he was using words.'

THE CITY

THE CITY by Stephen Crowe ©2013 www.invisibledot.net

The Run of the Streets
Karl Whitney

I close the door of the apartment and duck through the corridors, under the low wooden beams, down the stairs past the post boxes on which the names of the inhabitants of the building are printed; one of them reads 'Bastard'.

I press the button to release the heavy front door and I'm out on the street. Suddenly, Parisian life teems around you, like the volume has just been turned up. Like you've just been underwater and have quickly surfaced.

I set off at pace along the street, dodging past the tables of the small cafés that adjoin our building. I pass the small community garden on the corner, cross the small side street and run in the direction of the traffic lights at the top of the street. Trousseau, Charles Delezcluse, Charonne: these are the three streets that I've so far intersected on my run from the apartment in the 11th Arrondissement.

On 3rd December 1851, at the southern end of rue Trousseau, Alphonse Baudin, a deputy in the French Assembly, was shot dead on a barricade that had been erected after the previous day's seizure of power by Louis Napoleon. On the wall of a building nearby, a plaque whose text is etched in gold paint commemorates his death.

Paris is a city upon which so many layers of history can be read that sometimes it can seem not a living and breathing city at all, but rather an archive of past events and people and ideas that have been lived out on such a grand scale that, for those who live there, it can surely appear difficult to do anything new or worthwhile.

It didn't seem that way to me, though—although the place I had just come from, Dublin, had begun to wrap itself around me like a shroud. For me, Paris was an escape —another way of seeing.

I needed to leave Dublin. But I knew I'd have to go back. In the time between leaving Dublin and returning to it I began, seriously, to work on a book about the Irish capital. Most of this work was done in Paris, and when I wasn't writing, or thinking about writing, I ran.

I cross the curving rue de Charonne, whose jagged building plots hint at its medieval origin and distract momentarily from the straight lines of Haussmann's boulevards.

When I begin my run I'm always aware of the awkwardness of my body—my legs don't move in the way that I'd like and my arms are held too high, or, when I realise my arms are too high, I overcompensate by holding them too low. Then some residual soreness from a past run reveals itself. I often use this soreness as first a bogeyman to scare me off completing my run, and then a straw man to be easily defeated—'see? I kept going, even though I felt awful when I started.'

So I'd run. And while I was running I would often think about Raymond Queneau.

Queneau was born in Le Havre in 1903. He arrived in Paris as a student and remained there for the rest of his life. When I picture Queneau, I see the multiple passport-sized prints of the young writer, hair long on top and short on the sides, caught in a variety of comic poses: one where his head is bent forward while he ruffles his hair, another where his round glasses that sit askew are about to fall from the bridge of his nose. In others he adopts monstrous faces that barely mask his laughter.

Whereas Queneau's Paris—the area in which he lived and the place he wrote most about—was located to the west of the city, I was drawn to the east. That's where the apartment I shared with my girlfriend was, that's where the library I worked in stood. So when I ran out the door of my apartment building and thought about Queneau's Paris, I was translating it from west to east: to the storefront petrol stations and pizza joints of the area near place de la Nation. But, as I ran, I was also thinking about the way, in the early 1930s, when work was hard to come by for Queneau as for many others, he picked up a job writing a tiny column for a newspaper. Each day, three, often cryptic, questions about Paris would turn up in *L'Intransigent* under the heading 'Connaissez-vous Paris?' The following day, the answers would be printed below three more questions, and so on. Queneau wrote the column between November 1936 and October 1938, after which he got a job at the publisher Gallimard as a reader.

Here's an example of Queneau's style: on Christmas Day 1936, the following question was asked in the column:

'What is the deepest point in the Metro?'

(This question made me laugh when I first read it, because its phrasing—'the deepest' is 'le plus profonde'—seems to lend the underground spot an existentialist cool.)

The next day, the answer appeared:

'Between Abbesses and Lamarck, Metro line 12 passes 62 metres below the level of the rue Norvins.'

The more one reads of Queneau's Paris trivia, the more it exhibits a craftily ludic sensibility of the sort shown by the jigsaw-maker Gaspard Winckler in Georges Perec's *La vie mode d'emploi*. Queneau, who would later form the Oulipo group of which Perec would be a member, was playing games with the reader, and with the city.

Running to me has never been a natural thing. At school, I failed to take up any sports convincingly—I scored own goals when playing football, I never got to grips with the wholly alien sport of basketball and once, when learning how to swim, I jumped into a pool, hurt my back, thought I was drowning and never returned.

With sport I never saw the point. But while I pursued this querulous relationship with sporting endeavour my mother had become a runner and was beginning to take part in marathons. Once, just after the Chernobyl nuclear disaster had happened, my mother, my brother, my uncle Declan and I travelled from our home in Dublin to Belfast on the train. It was the day of the Belfast marathon and, while she ran the course, we—my brother, my uncle and I —wandered around the redbrick, rain-streaked city. We saw armoured vehicles, and a park. On the train home, which was smoky with strong tobacco and dank like an old pub, my uncle drank a dark pint of Guinness.

So I was always aware of running. It was always around me—familiar, even—but I had never really considered it as something to do for its own sake. I always thought it a by-product of other things. Walking was something you did when you had to get somewhere; running was something you did when you had to get somewhere faster. You'd run if you were trying to get a bus, for example: you see the bus, you run.

You struggle. You miss the bus.

Maybe I should have started running much earlier: I missed a lot of buses.

So sometimes walking isn't enough. When I've walked around a city for some time, and I seem to have exhausted the possibilities of that place, I look for other approaches. I want to find an angle that will break open the city and reveal something else, something I haven't seen before.

That's how, when I came to write extensively about Dublin, I needed to hear other voices—people who would tell me things I didn't already know. But I also wanted to find other ways of getting around the city. As part of my research I had walked the twenty or so kilometres around what I somewhat arbitrarily decided were the boundaries of Tallaght, the oversized new town in south-west Dublin that had been my childhood home. While walking provided me with a speed and perspective that attuned me to the basic rhythms of the city, I also knew that walking was but one way of experiencing urban space.

I wanted to explore other ways of getting around. Around a year after my walk around Tallaght, I was living in Paris—travelling to the Bibliothèque Nationale, the French National library, to sit at my laptop computer on which I tried to write more about Dublin, in the hope that what I wrote would slot together to form a book about my home town, and that the emails I sent out to agents, editors and journalists would elicit the kind of responses that would help convince me that what I was doing in writing about Dublin was achievable.

While sitting in the vast steel and glass subterranean reading rooms of the library, I thought of Joyce, certainly, and his time spent in Paris writing about Dublin, which became in his imagination a kind of mnemonic labyrinth through which the ghosts of his old acquaintances and enemies shuffled. But I also thought, again, of Raymond Queneau, who while writing his column for *L'Intransigeant* spent cold winter afternoons in the wood-lined reading rooms of the French capital's libraries, seeking arcane facts about Paris.

To get to the library from my home I would walk from the apartment to Ledru-Rollin Metro station, take a line 8 train to Daumesnil station, change for line 6 and clatter across the raised railway bridge that passes between the concrete promontory of the offices of the French Finance ministry and the pyramidal Bercy sports centre.

I bought a monthly ticket that allowed me to jump on and off buses and trains whenever I wanted. This was a freedom I didn't have in Dublin, and I investigated bus routes and railway lines around the city as much as I could: that year I bounced around the multi-coloured circuitry of the RATP Metro map.

The first time I got to Paris, I had booked tickets there on a whim. I was in my early twenties and had just left university. I had been in Belgium for a few days, but wanted to go somewhere else. For a small sum I was able to get a seat on a train from Brussels to Paris Gare du Nord, and from there wandered to a moderately filthy hostel that had no vacancies, but whose staff were able to direct me to a completely filthy hostel on the other side of the city. The other hostel had a single space: a mattress thrown on the floor of a bare room. I didn't care. I spent a day walking all over the city, only able to judge distances between places once I had paced them. This was the way to see Paris, I thought, somewhat romantically. But the next day I couldn't walk—at least not very far. The soles of my feet had blistered, and my legs were sluggish from the previous day's efforts.

I bought a tourist pass for the Metro, and, rather than going back to my mattress in the hostel, spent the rest of my time in the city travelling on its trains.

Raymond Queneau loved the Parisian bus system, and would sketch in his journal the routes his journeys on public transport took. I flicked through the pages of the published journals in the Bibliothèque Nationale, looking at the reproduced diagrams tracing the trajectories Queneau had taken around the city's streets—a walk, then a bus journey, then another walk. His movement through the city wasn't merely a nostalgic exercise in flâneurie, nor a Situationist-style utopian critique of modern urban form—rather it was, on some level, his attempt to understand the rhythms of Paris, rhythms generated by bus, train, motor car and foot. Queneau's characters are constantly in motion, even when they should be sitting still—in a kind of modernist slapstick that often reminded me of the windmilling hyperactivity that takes place in the films of Preston Sturges or Howard Hawks.

Zazie longs for the Metro; the banal incident that's re-told many times in *Exercises in Style* takes place on a Parisian bus. Car journeys, excursions in vans: everything moves in Queneau's kinetic fiction.

Queneau was not beyond his own spin on psychogeography: once, he walked with musician and novelist Boris Vian to an unfashionable industrial area on the left-bank—not far from the present site of the towering National Library—in order to look at a particularly weird street.

I run up avenue Ledru-Rollin, past an empty office block and a couple of bars: one a local *tabac*, the other a quasi-hipster establishment with an English name. My run brings me to place León Blum, where a statue of the Socialist leader and former Prime Minister regards the traffic on boulevard Voltaire through the non-existent lenses of his round glasses, his scarf permanently fixed at an angle as if blowing in the breeze.

I take a sharp right at McDonald's, past a casually-built fruit stall—merely a couple of crates on top of which the stall owner had arranged melons and bananas in order to snag hungry people emerging from the nearby Metro entrance. On occasion, when running past later in the evening, I would see the stall—well, the crates—left unmanned. Clearly no one touched them or moved them apart from the stall's owner.

The pavements of the boulevard Voltaire are broad—as broad as some streets—and a pleasure to run along. They're wide enough to have plenty of room to navigate around people walking slowly, people running slowly, people pushing buggies, people walking dogs, people on skateboards, and moped-riding pizza-delivery drivers with their crash helmets tipped upwards to allow them unobscured vision as they seek an unfamiliar address.

I'm getting into some sort of stride now—the stretch of boulevard Voltaire I run along is just over a mile, and uninterrupted by any major intersection. I pass the hotel which was the first address the young Picasso lived at in Paris. Just after this hotel, I would often see a tiny child's tricycle locked to a street sign. It could have been easily picked up and carried into a building by a parent, but instead it was tethered on the side of the street as if it were a much larger bicycle. I chose to regard it as an example of the kind of informal surrealism often generated unintentionally by Parisian streets.

Around the corner from the tricycle is the gymnase Japy, where, in 1899, the first formal meeting of French socialist organisations took place. Later, during the Second World War, the building was used to hold Parisian Jews who had been rounded up by the police and were about to be sent to the camps.

Near the gymnase Japy, a little further along the boulevard Voltaire, an entrance leads down to the Charonne Metro station. On 8 February 1962, a demonstration against the Algerian War made its way along the boulevard. Police blocked the protest before charging at the crowd. Chased by police, some protestors took shelter in the stairwells of the Metro station, at which point police hurled the heavy iron plates from the bases of nearby trees down the staircase. Nine people died as a result of the police's actions. Eight of them were Communist Party members or trade unionists.

On the fiftieth anniversary of the Charonne incident, I walked to the station and looked at the plaque commemorating the people who died. It was surrounded by floral bouquets which had been laid at a ceremony earlier that day.

No city is neutral. Paris is charged up with a radical past that refuses to disappear.

I run further, faster—to get away from Charonne Metro station, past which I couldn't run, through which I couldn't travel, without thinking of the dead protestors, or of the event that preceded it, when, in October 1961 the Parisian police had killed as many as 200 Algerian demonstrators, leaving their bodies to float along the Seine past Notre Dame cathedral.

Running through Paris, or, at least, running through the 11th and 12th arrondissements—the historically working class and radical areas in the east of the city—these points of conflict and hatred are barely hidden behind the pristine stone facades of the buildings and below the tarmac covering the paving stones of the boulevard.

One of the things I realised as I ran along boulevard Voltaire was that Paris was not my city—nor would it ever be. It was a melancholy realisation.

Another of the things I realised: Dublin was my city, whether I lived there or not. No matter how many times I left Dublin, I would always be drawn back, even if only through memories of the place. This also saddened me, but for different reasons: I was ambivalent about my home town. I loved and hated it in equal measure.

I knew that once I left Paris I'd return to Dublin. But once I returned to Dublin, I didn't know how long I'd remain there. As it happened, it wasn't very long.

In Dublin I continued to work on my book about the city. I wanted to write about Dublin's transportation system, which was routinely maligned. As it was mostly dependent on buses—its extensive tram system was torn up in the mid-twentieth century—and Dublin's traffic was often heavy, public transportation in the city had acquired a reputation as being slow and poorly integrated.

How to write about this unheroic, unprepossessing transport system? I thought about what Raymond Queneau might do, then tried to plan a system whereby I would jump on and off buses over a set period of time, then see where I would end up. In this way, the bus would help me to generate a non-fiction narrative about the city, and I would merely transcribe it. Except that it wasn't that simple: by defining constraints—how long I would spend on each bus, whether I would stay at the same stop or cross the road to get one travelling in the opposite direction—I had at least a degree of control over the system.

In the process, I discovered another way of writing about dear old overfamiliar Dublin—a method that, it now seems to me, wouldn't have been possible without the time spent running around Paris thinking about Queneau's work.

I was almost home—having left the apartment I had run in a triangular pattern across east Paris and was heading northwards below the old overhead tracks of the railway, recently transformed into a linear park.

Near the intersection of avenue Ledru-Rollin and rue du Faubourg St Antoine, I recalled the scene near the beginning of Jean-Luc Godard's 1964 film *Bande à Part*, where the actress Anna Karina, playing a character called Odile, cycled through this intersection, heading in the direction of Bastille. Passing the Monoprix supermarket, she hopped off her bike before turning down a nearby alleyway to a building where her character was about to attend a language class.

Godard's film captured some of the antic lunacy of Queneau's early fiction, and indeed a copy of his 1937 novel *Odile* makes an appearance at one point, thumbed by the kind of seedy gangsterish characters that could have walked out of the pages of his books.

Perhaps these scenes in this film, capturing as they did a place familiar to me, were what drew my thoughts towards Queneau and his work as I ran through the streets. When I think about the anticipation of crossing this intersection, of its associations with Godard's film and by extension Queneau's novel, it helps to remind me that a place can have all manner of strange resonances that continue to act on you long after you've moved on.

I went back to Dublin and got on the bus.

Speeds & Shapes of Consciousness
An Interview with Evan Lavender-Smith by David Winters

On the strength of two short books—each slim enough to be read in a single sitting—Evan Lavender-Smith has established himself as one of America's leading literary artists: a writer whose work reconfigures the relations between fact and fiction, form and content, writing and reading. Not only this, but Lavender-Smith speaks as much to philosophers as to lovers of literature. His books have been copiously praised by some of the most pioneering voices in contemporary fiction (Gary Lutz, Brian Evenson, Michael Martone) and by prominent scholars of continental thought and critical theory (Clare Colebrook, John Mullarkey, and Ian Buchanan, among others). Lavender-Smith's first book, *From Old Notebooks* (BlazeVox, 2010; Dzanc, 2012) presents a constellation of self-reflexive fragments—scattered thoughts on writing, thinking, and the comic chaos of family life—that combine to create a vivid, living literary meditation, reminiscent of Montaigne and David Markson. His second book, *Avatar* (Six Gallery Press, 2011) treads strikingly different territory: recalling Bernhard and the late works of Beckett, this grief-crazed monologue gives us a glimpse of life at its limit, stranded in space, left only with tears, stray strands of hair, and degraded memories for company. Taken together, these two texts testify to a level of intellectual and aesthetic adventurousness rarely seen in recent literature. Evan and I corresponded by email throughout September 2013, in a conversation that ranged from the legacy of modernism to the vital importance of style and form for both literary and philosophical writing.

DW Forgive me for beginning with some fairly broad brushstrokes. Reading both of your books together, my first instinct is to try to make comparisons between the two. This may be a mistake on my part (I'm not sure why two texts' shared authorship should automatically make them candidates for comparison) but perhaps there are commonalities. For instance, both books present what we could call the 'rhythm of thought.' But each book is driven by a different rhythm—most rudimentarily, that of the fragment on the one hand, and the unbroken monologue on the other. So, to start with, I'm interested in how you conceive of the relationship between these two modes, and the capacity of each to reflect (or rather, produce?) 'thought'…

ELS It seems that my own thought often proceeds in one of those two ways, either in the mode of the concise fragment (e.g. 'Need eggs') or in the mode of the excessive interior monologue (e.g. 'Eggs eggs Walmart today tomorrow eggs must buy them don't forget the eggs…'). I've spent a lot of time trying to really think about the way I think, but I'm still not sure that I have a very good handle on it. I listen to myself think; invariably I forget what I've heard, so I return to the most basic questions. *Do I think in words? If so, what type of syntax is involved?* These are the simple, first-order questions; it gets trickier when the relationship between thought and writing is introduced. *How is (or isn't) language/writing commensurable to thought?* What might a formalist representation of thought look like, in contrast to a realist representation of thought? That last question has particularly interested me, the possibility of non-realist literary forms reflecting the hidden or forgotten rhythms and syntaxes of thought. As to your point about the literary mode producing rather than merely reflecting thought, yes, of course, at a certain point it's six of one, half a dozen of the other: I perceive my words and sentences feeding off other words and sentences in the same way I perceive my thoughts feeding off other thoughts; I intuit a certain immanence about content, as determined by form, just as I perceive a certain immanence about thought, as determined by the body. I don't know that the language's self-generative ability is any more marked in the fragmentary mode as it is in the monologic mode; it seems to be a fundamental feature of both modes, or of any mode in which I write, including the rambling mode of the answer to the interview question.

DW Insofar as 'non-realist' representations of thought reveal what is 'forgotten' by realism, they sometimes seem to refine as much as they refute the classical realist aesthetic. In conversation with Arthur Power, Joyce declared that *Ulysses* had opened up 'a new orientation in literature—the new realism.' One finds similar statements in Woolf's essays. Generalising, perhaps some of the more extreme experiments in modernist formalism still pursue a mimetic goal, aiming for a greater realism than that of realism. In *From Old Notebooks* you call Joyce out for *Ulysses*' 'conceit'—as you say, 'people don't actually think that way!' Yet you praise *Ulysses* as that rare innovation, a 'novel that really thinks about thinking.' If Joyce's project was to portray the *reality* of thought, is this, then, a challenge (perhaps doomed by definition) that you think today's writers should rise to?

ELS Not necessarily, no. Although I do see a challenge facing today's writer that may be bound up with the project of literary modernism in a more general way. As it was, that realism emerged in the final decades of the twentieth century as a dominant mode of Anglophone literary expression, much as it had early in the twentieth century preceding the advent of what we commonly think of as the heyday of literary modernism, certain of today's writers may feel dissatisfied with or dispossessed by this second reign of realism, and they may feel compelled to overcome it by parodying dominant literary modes or attempting to invent new ones. I certainly feel that challenge from time to time, especially when I muster the courage to glance at the contents page of the *NYT Book Review*.

As it pertains to Joyce, I would take issue with a portrayal of *Ulysses* as a book in which the 'reality of thought' is present. First, and obviously, what we think of as the 'realist' mode of *Ulysses*, what Joyce called its 'narrative' mode—the mode of the first chapter, for example, at the tower, or the mode of the fourth chapter, at 7 Eccles St.—is simply not present in many of the novel's chapters. And second, even when Joyce employs this mode—alternating chronologically or etiologically or associatively between dialogue and character-pressurised narratorial reportage and character-based interior monologue—the mode remains, to my reading, fundamentally formalist, as it is that the author constructs rigorous formal rules for narrative from which he attempts not to deviate, narratological rules for the representation of life and thought that possess perhaps merely an analogous or isomorphic relationship to the conditions of real-life life and thought. Bloom's thought, for example, as lingualised and syntacticised by Joyce, is a thoroughly and rigorously contrived narratological object, unlike anything we experience in life. But what makes the writing most profoundly non-realist, to my mind, is that it's also unlike anything we ever experience in the so-called realist novel. Joyce is rigorous and meticulous in his creation of an intensity of formal immanence wholly unique to his novel's semiotic regime—even, amazingly, to each individual chapter's semiotic regime—to an extent that makes the novel seem able to escape any aesthetic or generic pigeonholing we might try to inflict on it. The book's formal mode is Joyce, its genre is Joyce… When I use *realism* to describe a form of literary writing, I may be referring less to a novel's attempts at mimesis than I am to a set of narratological conventions, which, over time, have become familiar to writers and readers of novels and therefore have gained a certain efficacy despite possessing little rigour or little if any contemporary applicability. *It was so realistic*, as a reader's response to a novel, generally translates to, *It conformed to the historical conventions of prose narrative so shrewdly.*

You cite Woolf and say that the most extreme modernist formal experiments generally pursue mimesis—I would point to Woolf's own *The Waves* as a powerful counterexample, a novel in which a narrative treatment of character and language and thought largely turns its back on mimetic representation for the sake of perspectival and linguistic and noological discovery and insight, a novel that, to my reading, more or less renders the whole realism—realer realism oneupmanship conversation moot. I would say the same of much of Beckett's later writing. This is where I often finally land when thinking about mimesis in relation to narrative, a return to my desire for difference, for stranger configurations of language and form that would seem wholly out of place in that mimetic mode we commonly associate with the contemporary/nineteenth-century realist novel.

DW Right. I agree that the resurgence of familiar realist *conventions* in recent mainstream fiction is depressing. Sometimes, though, I simply want to soften this 'realism/modernism' distinction—at least insofar as the destruction of such conventions could itself constitute (and has at times been conceived as) an *approach* to the real, or a remodeling of it.

But you cut to the crux of what matters to me as a reader when you talk about form producing an intensity that seems 'unique' or singular to the work. Sontag once said that 'in art, content is…the pretext, the lure which engages consciousness in essentially formal processes of transformation.' For me, this phrase could apply not only to 'art' or fiction, but also to philosophy—where my comprehension of the propositional content seems almost secondary to the experiential, emotive, cathectic connection I might feel with the form.

That's pretty much how I felt when reading *From Old Notebooks*. It's also how I feel when reading, for instance, Lars Iyer's books. The book presents an abundance of intellectual material that for me functions as a 'lure'; it's alluring (I'm thinking of your line about Markson: 'porn for English majors') yet the heart of my reading experience really isn't quite *there*, it's elsewhere: it's more in the way the form frames and transforms that material, and maybe, then, it's in the way that transformation transforms me. This is also the way I read, say, Deleuze or Adorno—less for the intellectual content of the text than for the transformative effect of its *texture*. Do you feel any affinity with what I'm fumbling towards here?

I do, yes. This is a bit different from what you're describing, but I remember reading Derrida and becoming aware of the fact that I wasn't really making any substantive leap from the words on the page to extra-textual referents, to anything out there in the world, and yet I was still very much desiring the continuation of the text, the extension of the text's form in my mind. It seemed like I'd gained access to a secret or interior meaning, an alternate mode of reading and meaning-making in which the words accrued to refer to or establish some intra-textual formal intensity or truth. In Markson—*Reader's Block*, say—there's always a point when the content begins to blur, when I've relaxed my vision of the novel's surface in order to project my attention below or behind the language, to engage more viscerally with the novel's form. Of conceptualism in general one might say that gestures of appropriation and repetition invite the reader to look past or beyond content and instead toward form and production. **ELS**

Maybe it's important to note that these experiences are different from, but perhaps related to, the experience of 'spacing out' while reading. Right now I'm reading Tolstoy, and I find myself regularly spacing out, by which I mean I'll be reading along and tracking the content when all of a sudden I'll notice that I haven't been tracking the content for the last paragraph or two, sometimes even the last page or two, that I've sort of fallen into a hole in my own mind, maybe thinking about what's for dinner, when was the last time I had tilapia for dinner, imaginary etymologies for the word *tilapia*, for the word *dinner*, etc. I'm sure I space out while reading for a variety of reasons; what interests me about spacing out while reading in relation to the Derrida and Markson reading experiences, as described above, is the possibility of engaging in a kind of double activity while reading. During my most memorable, powerful reading experiences, I was doing one thing that led to another thing; I was engaging with the content of the book when for one or another reason I felt compelled to engage with it in a different, additional way, perhaps in a more visceral way or a more corporeal way, perhaps in a more 'personal' way.

Maybe this is just a fancy way of reframing or intellectualising the reader's familiar claim that she had 'fallen' or 'escaped' into something called 'the world of the book.' I suppose the difference here, with respect to the Derrida and Markson reading experiences, is that the 'world of the book' is more closely aligned with the book's form—perhaps its 'texture,' as you call it—than with its immediate content, with Markson's specific anecdotes or Derrida's specific abstractions. When I fall into the world of a Markson novel, I'm not picturing myself in some dilapidated Brooklyn flat surrounded by thousands of note cards each containing a single death-related literary anecdote; instead, I've become less interested in the anecdotes themselves, more interested in the rhythms of their presentation and my reception of those rhythms, their syntactic rhythms, of course, but also those rhythms I associate simply with the application of my consciousness to the book, or with the speeds and shapes of my consciousness as revealed by the book—with the form of the book and with the book's formal effects on me.

As a younger reader, I think I perceived a gap or disproportion between what I imagined to be my 'comprehension'—my focus on the writing's immediate content—and my 'desire'—my yearning for experiences of formal intensity—as indicative of a shortcoming on my part, maybe of my impatience or my overambition as a reader. Now I would say that I actively seek out reading experiences in which I perceive rifts and doublings in my attention, and, as it sounds like you are, I'm especially interested in such a thing happening during my reading of philosophy. I tried to talk about it a bit in *From Old Notebooks* as a 'sensation' associated with reading that follows from certain rhythms established by the text—syntactic rhythms, structural rhythms, etc. I suppose there is something musical about reading a work of philosophy and allowing its 'intellectual content' to recede a bit so this more visceral experience of form can take hold—it does seem similar to the way I listen to certain types of music. When I think about my reading of Wittgenstein's *Tractatus*, for example, I certainly don't first think about any specific brilliant insight associated with a certain proposition in the book; instead I think of something like the book's aura, maybe the way its aura marked me as a reader.

If I do think more specifically about the book, I would likely think about specific movements of form: the book's early insistence on logic and immanence giving way to later revelations of lyricism and transcendence; in short, I would think of the book's beauty. It doesn't seem to me that this is a way philosophers like to talk about philosophy; even self-described 'meta-' philosophy or 'anti-' philosophy focuses mostly on problems associated with philosophy's 'claims' or 'subjects.' Philosophers sometimes seem to forget that they're writing books, that they're talking about books; they seem to want to pretend that they're just talking about ideas. Of course, it may also be that I'm a bit more bibliocentric than the philosopher's implied reader, that reader who would imagine the book as a mere container for ideas, as opposed to a means or machine for the production of ideas. I have a hard time imagining the possibility of a philosophy that hasn't been shaped by pressures of aesthetic formalisation. Can philosophy exist beyond, or prior to, form? I can't imagine what such a thing would look like. In *From Old Notebooks*, there are several cheeky references to the tunnel vision of philosophers with respect to this stuff, but the call for an aesthetics of philosophy was, I believe, made in earnest, for the very reason you describe: philosophy's most powerful effects often reside in the more obscure formal recognitions made by the reader, not necessarily in the writing's declarative, denotative philosophical propositions.

DW Yes; in some respects, perhaps reconstructing those propositions in purely epistemic terms isn't really 'reading' them at all, since real reading is rife with the imperfections of *living*. Readers err, 'space out,' skip and stall; as Barthes puts it, a reader's attention imprints 'abrasions' upon the text. And relatedly, as you say, reading can involve intuition as much as tuition—an idea, once read, isn't just an idea, but an associative node, as affective and aesthetic as it is intellectual.

So, in this kind of reading experience, it seems like writing's form or style is the site of its intersection with *life*. It's almost as if, through form, something living is folded into writing. Then, in our encounter with that form—our skewed, errant 'reading' of it—this implicit life is animated; vivified. Or rather, writer and reader each enter into a *shared* lifeworld, one that arises from within the formal 'world of the book.'

Crucially though, the kind of 'life' constructed by a book isn't reducible to the biographical lives that collide with it. For instance, the narrator of *From Old Notebooks* shares various autobiographical details with you, the author. But the book's own subjectivity seems to exceed autobiography—am I right about that? I wonder whether you have any thoughts on the different 'forms of life' that might be produced in the process of writing and reading—in your work and elsewhere.

ELS I think I tend to associate autobiography, even 'content' in general, primarily with the past, whereas I often think about style and form in relation to the future. Content has already happened, it already exists in a condition of being; form is always becoming, always in a condition of vergency. I like to imagine the possibility of a book's content—be it autobiography, detective narrative, whatever—as little more than an occasion for style, for the evolution of style. Another way of saying that the book's subjectivity 'exceeds autobiography' may be to say that the book is looking to style or form, rather than content, rather than 'life's events,' for answers to those same questions regularly posed by autobiographical investigation, questions like *Who am I?* or *Why am I here?* I've tried to answer those questions in a less humanist, and hopefully in a more honest, way: *I'm the author of the book. I'm here to discover the formal possibilities of the book, to write toward the book's future.*

I often feel as though I'm attempting to distill life into these little puzzles or puddles or piddles of language that bear a kind of isomorphic or formal resemblance to life's conditions and forms. One of the things I most like as a reader is the feeling of being *reminded of life* while reading— not necessarily seeing or hearing familiar manifestations of life, maybe instead feeling structures and forms in language that resemble structure and form as I've come to know them through life. I think I probably first experienced a recognition along these lines while reading metafiction, maybe reading Coover when I was young and getting this eerie feeling that the book somehow contained another, hidden book inside it, a book that wasn't quite available to my reading but was still somehow there, below the surface of the book at hand. There was the book and its structures, first, then there was something else within the book that reminded one of the book's structures, that resembled those structures.

I feel this way in Borges all the time, and it remains the great pleasure of Borges for me, being reminded of structure, being reminded of structure-as-such. Of course I'm using 'reminded' in a way that I hope doesn't suggest what I want as a reader is a depiction or a 'picture' of life that I already possess, life's verisimilitude as minutely rendered by the novel somehow corresponding to my own memories, etc. Rather, what I desire most of all is the implication of life and the structures of life; I enjoy feeling an opaque, elliptical intensity about the relationship between the structures and forms in what I'm reading or writing and the structures and forms I've encountered in my so-called real life, in my biological life, my political life, my amorous life, etc. I suppose I want to be reminded, simply, mysteriously, that structure and form exist in the world. Why it is I desire this, I'm not exactly sure; it may be that seeing life estranged and reconfigured in language offers some hope that life as we know it through experience—mundane life, mere life—isn't necessarily phenomenologically or definitionally limited to that experience; perhaps there are other paradigms of life and structure available for us to think and live. I often feel menaced by my perception of life's final total vacuity and irrelevance; art can sometimes introduce the possibility of an alternate reading of life, or it can sometimes confirm my menacing reading of life in a hopeful way—maybe through humour, as it often does in Bernhard's novels.

DW For me, parts of *Avatar* read almost like a thought experiment about the destruction—or at least, the erosion—of everyday lived experience. Certainly, there's a sense of an eroded consciousness—a consciousness which, over an almost inconceivable span of time, has undergone a complex process of experiential decay; a kind of cognitive heat death, perhaps. One aspect of the narrator's condition is that the words with which he makes sense of his world have come uncoupled from their referents—apparently as a result of extreme repetition. 'I had reached,' he reflects, 'my sixty-eight thousand nine hundred and sixty-eighth repetition of thinking of speaking the word pinecone.' Well, we're all familiar with this kind of thing on a far smaller scale (I just looked it up, and learned that it's called 'semantic satiation'). The way I read *Avatar*, it seemed as if something similar, albeit more exorbitant, had somehow set in across the full spectrum of the narrator's experience.

I wondered whether I could ask you to talk more about the narrative consciousness of *Avatar*; about the motives and/or methods behind its construction. And I suppose the last thing I want to ask, too, would be about the remarkable treatment of the concept of 'friendship' over the course of that narrative—a concept which appears to start out in the 'uncoupled' state I tried to describe above, but finally finds itself, it seems, complicated and transformed.

ELS I imagine the narrator possessing a kind of nostalgia for meaning, maybe for a world in which the relationship between language and experience is a bit less fraught. This is something I can identify with; I often desire a return to a condition I associate with adolescence, maybe with pre-adolescence, one in which the world's meaning doesn't seem quite so exhausted by language. At a certain point, around the age of twelve or so, language stopped illuminating the world's mystery and instead began chipping away at it, secularising it; I wonder if the narrative condition of *Avatar* isn't somehow related to the crisis of that transition. I'm sure a lot of the stuff in there about words becoming untethered from the things they're supposed to reference has as much or more to do with the erosion of mystery as it does with that of consciousness. Also, as you say, there's the absence of lived experience: I think it's fairly clear that the narrative condition is one in which experience has become more or less exclusively mental, one in which the body and physical sensation have become somewhat detached from mental experience, as if the experience of physical sensation has become more or less prosthetic, or as if we're limited to these very slight movements of fingers and eyeballs and hair follicles, etc.

But there is this one seemingly redemptive thing, as you mention, the possibility of friendship, the suggestion that mystery or salvation is still possible by way of the friend, that perhaps the engagement with a friend offers a kind of escape hatch from the dull horror of the narrator's existence. Of course he's forced to invent substitutes for friends—tears and strands of hair, etc.—as it is he's alone with his own mind, no real friends available to him, etc. But nonetheless, the concept of the friend is redemptive. I myself have few friends—I'm afraid I don't make a particularly good friend—but I still seem to take solace in the concept or the possibility of friendship, the silly thought that perhaps one day I'll learn to be a good friend, or, better, that someone who doesn't care how shitty a friend I am will come along and befriend me, save me, save my soul or something. I think that's probably what *Avatar*'s narrator is holding out for, as well, redemption of some kind, perhaps by way of the friend—but of course that redemption isn't really coming. The best the narrator can do, perhaps the best any of us can ever do, is invent some good imaginary terms for salvation.

Six Poems from {Enthusiasm}

S.J. Fowler

GREAT SCANDAL CATCHES

for James Byrne

if the cold meze is cold food what shall
we do while we wait? cry about it—under
it, well if we can afford a house in Holland
park I'm not sure I have a right to reminisce
in horror at what James described as slave
punishment, when Hector was forced to shit
in the other one's mouth, after all those who
remained celebrated, long after the fact
would it happened so often, and is so essential
to woman + man it's impossible to begin
at making sense of it. To which I'll say I
imagine every single incident of disembowelling
in a row, born again, born again, up with
the swamp water comes a myst & a music

Quidistant in 4 parts

for Sandeep Parmar

punishment trek to find the latest innocent
a way to market food to human minds that do
not possess hungry bodies up the up in
the hills with their distilleries brewing
out the clean + the clear because they're bored
well come finally to more of me & then that'll
fall aside because I won't be able to get to sleep
in the meantime it's tempting to copy + paste
the lyrics of Peter Gabriel + Kate Bush
don't give up cause you need that   flower
blood on the most modern phones travel
at an angle up, / child preaching childhood
sleep introduced to interruption, the black
bags before the eyes of children, later
weeks—the strain on Peter for he is great
the Great, dancing, hammer amidst the spray
the demented shine used to get that monsters
metal car so heavy solid looking new
weighing more than a polar bear
bluegrass to the very floor, I'm sorry you weren't
better welcomed but after all our jobs took you

M.I.T.

how doth fertiliser help the bomb? / &thus
how do I intend to help thee in thy plot to
airport > to airport another airport < another
more humanity for the planes, painted pink
dip them into sudden valleys where the giant
animals have miniaturised & the miniature
here become the land where technology is not
limited by anything & the imagination of flight
is apparently a mild head cold to the viral germ
warfare we ought suddenly employ when thinking
about what we might do with our future time
the end of fox hunting, the closure of steppe
fates _ .. that golden horde of disabled will no
longer be, their limbs straightened in the womb

BALMY

for the eclectic whip cracks children light
prostitute of the 80, lipstick, dressing gown
throats & event horizon, someone, burst in space
a film at the end of the street how one cut
the funeral for that friend who wouldn't go
is gone into the already known
the crust on its uppers, a bow on a box in west
acton is a human being learning to live in our world
paddington; the feet hardly moving
the fingers twitching to check our phone
I'm only just onto Paul Blackburn but I will
stay on him / I'm glad the venus nebula
is ever expanding because I'll not stop following
its expansion / there's always new & the catalogue
next to me can fuck off online where
man ray imagined women's mother milk well
well enough / love / hands between the feta crouch
for the greek pie / hard roast meat I hope to be
well dead before you run out gassing the oven
to invert those appreciating those working
who worked before the gas but now a shame
why did I watch the 4th *Underworld* film?
hot food, for hot food

Burn Museum

the gypsy wound
fighting man of a fighting family
bitterly pain full is a broken jaw, a bruised
kidney
it'll make you think twice, modern Paul
it doesn't just hurt, it's worse
it drifts its bookish suitcase
like a river of shirt toward work
a life of petty retreat, no more square
nose biting, not a real drift
& not too fair to go with them people
there are not enough to extinguish
to reflect how much hate there is
everywhere in every corner of living
a tomb of trinkets, a shackle
to the meaningless corrupt interpretation
of the recent past

BATH WITH MARLBOROUGH

If a baby dies in Bristol does it not rot
attracting maggots it does so why am I not
allowed to kill now before I've gone
in newcastle? standing outside the strip
deals working as a day, a door I see
4 bags + 1 bag & them a bottle go into
the boys face & run down + punch
the knifing boy in the ear, which rips
from the force of my punch but to him
the stabbed boy has been stabbed
in the linguistically & not the mock & he's
closing mam mam please help not to stall
me about jesus helping me mum my chest
burning grind me you don't know jesus
he can't pull the knife out but I am
& pull out the knife which is timing
& I later learn is a mistake & I got arrested
as the ear boy is 15 & I never work the door
again luck to not set a conviction

Killing Off Ray Apada
Matthew Jakubowski

The first time I saw Ray Apada he was standing outside the 7-Eleven near campus with no shirt, singing what I later found out were Muddy Waters songs he'd translated into Spanish and tried to adapt to twelve-string guitar. His voice was some kind of bad David Byrne impression but he could play guitar really well, keeping his eyes closed like he was completely into it, this six-foot-tall white dude built like a rock-climber with black hair buzzed short.

Next time I saw him he walked right by me on campus looking totally normal, wearing khakis, jean jacket, and a backpack.

'Hey, were you at a 7-Eleven playing guitar last Saturday? Half-naked?'

He stopped. 'You're the first person to say anything about that one. But you're right. That bare-chested thing was cheap. Not my usual performance protocol at all.'

He smiled. I must've looked dubious.

'No, really,' he said, 'I'm staging a bunch of emblematic public experiences right now. Have you heard of Pistoletto? The Italian artist who rolled a giant ball of newspaper through the streets of Turin in '68?'

Before I could speak he reached into his backpack and pulled out a sketch pad.

'Look, this is my schematic for a contemporary update of the ball. It's got microphones, speakers, cameras, and screens that will record every nearby image and sound, including audience commentary. So when I roll it across campus it will keep recording and broadcasting, reflecting everything around it, not just absorbing it like Pistoletto did, playing back all the sights and sounds that happen that day to the people who experience it.'

It was autumn, just a couple months before the presidential elections of 2000. Ray was in his junior year, like me. His dad was apparently a cello genius in a touring quartet with an international reputation and his mom had died when he was just a kid. 'It happened overseas,' he said, 'but I don't want to bore you with sad stories now.' Ray was on a music scholarship for classical guitar. In the semesters we hung out I met his friends Tristan, Leo, and Dave who gave him logistical help with his stunts. They weren't bad guys, just aloof with annoying habits that Ray never called them on, even when I made it obvious that they bothered me. Tristan liked to stare at people sometimes and say nothing when they spoke to him, even gave this one nice couple on the street the quiet treatment when they asked him how to get to the art museum. Leo and Dave talked in French way too much, which they knew me and Tristan didn't understand. But they were pretty serious about helping Ray goof off and Ray kept us from arguing with each other too much so we could actually accomplish a few things together.

They also didn't drink much, which was important to me back then. I'd had two girlfriends ditch me in eight months and it'd totally been my fault. Drying out for a little while sounded good, plus all I really had going for me at that point was a passion for a few German writers, a bunch of psych credits from my freshman year, and stacks of Musil and Broch to get through. I hadn't started hammering out any serious future plans. So Ray and his friends were a nice distraction, a lot more interesting than anyone else I'd met at school.

A month after I met them, I carried a fire extinguisher during Ray's one-man version of the Polish avant-garde theatre piece *Carmen Funebre* as he walked from the graduate library to the bell tower on painter's stilts bearing a fiery torch in one hand and cracking a bullwhip in the other. He did a lame stint as ManRayMan for three performances at coffeehouse open-mic nights where he'd stand barefoot, shouting at a photocopied picture of Walt Whitman, act terrified, knock over a table and flee. When it was freezing cold he told us to meet him at midnight on the hill near the arboretum's main entrance. When we got there, in reverence to all artistic sacrifice, lost in the magnitude of what our forebears had accomplished and the vision of who he hoped to be, he was spinning like a genuine dervish in full regalia—he'd hired someone in the theatre department to make the costume for him—and his bare white hands, purplish in the cold, described a circle as he cycled round and round, his head cocked toward the night sky, staring up into the moonlight. He fell over a few minutes later and I felt lucky to be able to applaud in front of the world and pick him up by his freezing hands, holding him close for a second, this weird brother I couldn't stop following around.

I started to feel like he might become a lifelong connection to greatness for me. He didn't care if hanging out with him wore you out and it didn't matter that he rarely took the time to offer so much as a thank you. But he kept doing and saying things that made me feel like I'd had a brush with the eternal, the kind of energy I'd always wanted to get closer to and merge with to flow towards better things. With Ray it was like traveling week to week with a different artistic guide, one day our happy Beat stereotype mad to live, the next day a bourgeois soldier, à la Flaubert's maxim to stay regimented in life and wild in our work. He got me seeing bigger things for myself. Ray seemed to have read everything; he feared Rimbaud, constantly wondered aloud if our times and society could have produced someone like Dostoyevsky, and loved Japanese literature, even got us all to read *Tale of Genji*. 'Japanese writing, I mean from Basho to Mishima, are you kidding me? We'll never get through it all alone. You'd need six lifetimes to read everything.' He wanted us to explore as much as he did, not so we could talk big, but to give each other tips on as many truly great things as we could before we graduated.

In January, Ray got what I thought was good news—he won the Tapper Award for student playwriting. He had submitted a work-in-progress called *Dynamo Blues*, a one-man show about his philosophy that no soul should pursue a single art. Ray had said many times that he'd never specialize, it just wasn't in his blood. 'That's what turned Gregor Samsa into a cockroach—society's pressure to specialize,' he'd said, and what killed Mozart was the need to make money, and every artist was wise to fear the limits imposed on them by the world in their era.

Winning that award didn't give Ray a big head, it had the opposite effect, but it definitely messed with the good connection we had going. A few days after he won he got banned from Levin's Books for shoving this little guy who said Beckett was overrated. A day later, Ray came to my apartment and said, 'That's it. From now on I'm a writer. I'm dropping everything else. Writing, only writing!'

I almost laughed, but he looked terrified, which scared me for reasons I didn't understand until many years later. If he was serious, this wouldn't be a small decision, since he was on a music scholarship.

I didn't question him about it right then, just tried to calm him down a little. 'Of course you're a writer,' I said, 'that's what you've always been.'

'This is a sign,' he said. 'Winning this prize happened for a reason.'

I told him I understood.

'You get it, right?' he said. 'To finish the play I have to focus on it and nothing else. I have to specialize for a little while, let my other stuff suffer.'

I remember how relieved I was to hear him say this. Even as a half-ass spectator to the things he did I was exhausted. Because of Ray I was behind in my readings and had also turned down a chance to work with a girl on a project that later got published in an anthology from a serious university press. I had no idea what kind of grades Ray was getting but assumed he was doing okay, though maybe in retrospect he'd actually failed some classes or been on academic probation. So it felt good to hear him confess that it was impossible to do quite so much and he might have to tone things down a bit. I was looking forward to a break. But I got roped back in a couple days later when Ray confided that he was having these almost catatonic fugue episodes every day, some lasting nearly two hours when he'd stare at the pens on his desk, or at his hands in his lap, worrying that he'd chosen the wrong art and was headed in a bad direction.

'I look at something and see it,' he said, 'then I blink and it's still there. I blink again and I thank God that it's still there, on and on like that, terrified the pattern might end.'

I told him to stay put and talk to me for a while.

He said he'd spoken to the music school dean and officially declined his scholarship. He also had an appointment with an advisor about changing his major. So that was it. All the work he'd put into studying music would probably amount to no degree and most likely there wouldn't be any more musical or theatrical stunts.

Though it was serious now, I was secretly, and suddenly, happy. I saw myself graduating before Ray, beating him in at least one way with a cheap victory. After all, he had his playwriting award. What did I have to show?

'You're doing the right thing,' I said.

'I know. It's what she'd want.'

'Who?'

I thought for a second that maybe all along there had been some girl he'd been dating who none of us knew about, someone who encouraged this big change of heart and urged Ray to throw away his scholarship. But a few minutes later he started telling me about his Mom and how she died. I had known about his Dad's music success, but I didn't know his Mom had been a writer. She'd started out as a biophysicist, earned a ton of money, then turned poet, traveled sometimes with her husband, wrote about the places they went, and published several essay and poetry collections. She was with her husband in 1992 after a concert in Bucharest and his next show was in Rome, so they decided to visit Medjugorje in what used to be Yugoslavia, where the Virgin Mary had been appearing for more than a decade. It was October, cold as hell in the mountains, and she caught pneumonia the day after they visited the hill where the spirit had descended and spoken so many times before. Open civil war was getting into full swing at the time and Ray's parents were stranded by some of the early fighting. They couldn't get her treatment.

'She died riding in the back of some car with my dad. He'd promised a guy ten thousand dollars if he could make it through the mortar fire and streets full of craters. But the war was too intense that day. It stopped them.'

Eleven-year-old Ray had been back home in Virginia at boarding school when she died.

We only spoke that one time about her death, but it was clear that of course he must've been holding back on blaming his dad's touring lifestyle for his mom's death, and that his parents' success had inspired him badly, to try and be as good as the both of them, rather than settling into one real thing he loved. We were already about three-quarters of the way through college and Ray just hadn't made the kind of splash he felt he had to being the child of two brilliant people. So now something in Ray had snapped under this decision to pursue writing, his mom's chosen art, all because he saw the playwriting prize as a direct sign to follow her and abandon music, his dad's art.

My theory, which I didn't have to tell him since I'm sure he knew it, too, was that there was some guilt or trauma connected to his mom's death that had to be expelled, so he could grieve properly like he needed to. I offered to help and he agreed to work together.

After a few back-and-forth discussions about possible methods that might work for us as amateurs to get at some of his anxieties, checking in of course with our texts on Jungian analysis and some of Freud's essays, we decided to use a simple approach to help him chill out, where he'd vent for as long as it took, in as much detail as possible, telling me his bad dreams, including any frantic daydreams and obsessive thoughts, all blended together, forgetting the truth—and I'd transcribe everything he said. I knew it would mean losing study time for side projects that might've helped me get into a good grad school, but I have to admit I was curious as hell to see how our plan would work out, knowing it might actually backfire and I'd get to see Ray break down, maybe witness this incredible mind deteriorating right in front of me. I could catch up later on my studying.

The goal was that once some of these particular demons were captured in words they'd be at his mercy, not vice-versa. He'd have them in another dimension besides thought and could mess with them in this realm the way he felt his memories of his mom were holding him captive.

We both knew he could've done something like this with a shrink, or done it by himself, but working together saved him time and cash. Since Ray had just abandoned his music scholarship his dad had cut him off of family money for a little while, so funds were tight.

Ray would talk, lying on the floor usually, while I typed quick as I could, transcribing things pretty much word-for-word on a laptop. We used this process for about two months and seven dreams. By the sixth and seventh dreams we had our technique down pretty well.

Here's the seventh and final transcript we made, starring Ray, as told to me by the man himself.

Ray Apada: Dreamdump #7: March 7, 2001:

I remember sitting with a crowd of people in the first few rows of a quiet theatre near the stage. It was late, about one in the morning. The lights in the theatre were low. The stage was dimly visible. There was this irritating tour guide man like a ringmaster who did a lot of talking in a wild but at the same time perfectly ordinary voice. I remember him talking about, or maybe I want to remember him saying something like, 'It is, after all, just a room with a great story,' and then going on about how the show he was producing was spiritually different than every other show that had ever existed before, that it was the best kind of show because his didn't progress, or change, except as a memory, as something we the people would remember later on as being better than the first time we all saw it together.

I think I remember thinking the guy was sort of crazed because he said the show we were about to watch was going to be quite violent and involve very real physical pain for several individuals in the audience, with hammers and sharp flying metal and flames and at that point a woman in the audience stood up looking scared, or pretending to be a damsel in distress so she could show off her sheer dress, barely veiling her black bra and panties.

The theatre guide laughed and said it was fine, there was no danger, he was just talking theoretically, so the woman sat back down again to some quiet laughter from her male companion and two other men in the group.

Then as the man kept talking, all I could think about was how transparent, lacy and quite appealing the whole idea of a perfect performance was. I remember a phrase like 'collective orgasm' right before the theatre man suddenly got really furious about some failure and shouted, 'It would've convinced the world, Matchmaker!' Which was hilarious to me and some other people in the crowd.

When the show started it was one actor in jeans and a t-shirt. Except below the rolled-up ends of his jeans I saw he wore very black socks made out of silk or something, and no shoes. The actor started reciting what was I think a poem. I remember looking from my seat through the rows of people and seeing the back of my mother's head as she first leaned over whispering to a man on her right, and later on leaned to whisper to a man on her left. I looked away from her toward the actor on stage and noticed that he sort of resembled me. (Okay, maybe it was me performing for my parents, trying to impress them. I get that).

When I looked back into the heads of the audience in the dark theatre I couldn't see my mom anymore. Then the actor started yelling a long rant and all I remember him saying was 'anguish' and 'a hand splashing water,' as he really beared down to scream, with his fists at his sides, then a lot of swear words before he repeatedly yelled 'adjust, adjust,' or maybe he said 'anguish' again, with his eyes wide open, turning his head toward each person in the audience one-by-one until it didn't even sound like a word anymore.

After the actor's little poem was over the stage lights went off and the house lights came on. The actor bowed once and walked away to the sound of us politely clapping.

My dad was back and asked us if we wanted drinks and everyone was standing in the aisle holding a wine glass or a whiskey glass or a martini. I remember wondering if the woman in the transparent clothes was worth talking to. I tried to get next to her but there was something going on with her and the two guys who had laughed when she had freaked out before, or pretended to freak out, and the tour guide was kind of hanging near her, too, protectively it looked like, or maybe just trying to get in the running, and I just felt alone and snubbed. What really made me decide to leave though is that at one point I looked at the stage and saw in the dimness off in the wings that the actor who had just performed was standing there like a corpse staring at us, either because he thought we couldn't see him, or because he was fully devoted to what this whole thing was about, but either way, I looked back and it seemed like he had seen me and was smiling at me for noticing him there.

I remember I didn't point him out to anyone else, even though I wanted someone to notice the guy, too, but I was too shy, and felt like I should have known that the theatre really is just a strange place after all. So I just put my whiskey on the end of one of the theatre seats, half-cushion, half-metal, facing upwards, kind of waved to the crowd who didn't stop talking or drinking to say good bye and I walked away up the aisle feeling like my life depended on me being strong enough not to look back toward the stage before I left. And I didn't.

That's the end of Ray's dream.

He never said much about the other transcripts we made, but the first time I printed this one out he read it and said, 'This classic method we're using is good. Confronting your memories lets you put destiny right there, dead center.' I didn't have time then to figure out what he meant exactly. I'd wasted weeks and needed to get serious about my classes. He had to finish his play so he'd get the Tapper Award money.

I didn't see him freak out again after we made those transcripts. He was less frantic and I felt like I'd helped him at a critical time, one of those clear-cut moments when a friend needs help and you think you can't, because of what you hold against him, but you actually manage to pull it off. We had drinks once or twice and he seemed good before the school year ended.

That summer, I worked painting houses as part of my uncle's business. Ray emailed me just once. 'This play is the best thing I ever worked on. I couldn't have done it without your help. Thanks, man.' I told him it was no problem, then did some complaining about how much my summer job sucked and mentioned a few grad schools I was thinking about applying to next year. He didn't write back that week or the week after. I wound up drinking more and more. That of course just made me feel worse. I should've been saving that beer money for school; unlike Ray, some of us didn't have family money to cover tuition and everything else.

I wrapped up my summer job with my uncle and was back in school by the end of August. Weeks went by and Ray wasn't around. Then 9/11 happened and I got a bit worried when Ray still wasn't returning calls or emails, even though I knew there was practically zero chance he'd died that day since he lived in Delaware with his dad at the time. This was confirmed when we got a broadcast message from our university president saying that only an alum had been killed, no one else from the school. I didn't have Ray's home number at his dad's, which made me feel stupid for not thinking of asking Ray for it before, and when I checked it wasn't listed in the student directory.

After the attacks, my folks said I should take a break from school if I needed to, but I stayed and studied hard, focusing in, sort of hoping my effort might conjure up Ray, and he'd reappear in the form of this great young writer, clean-shaven and ready to go and we'd patch things up with the old group, which had split up in some sort of post-9/11 freakout or something when everybody started boozing harder, dropping out, and hooking up pretty frantically with whoever they could and I went from having a decent crowd of people around me to almost no one.

Nobody from the old group really had anything to say when I asked them about Ray. I started to avoid them out of spite at first, then embarrassment for letting them get to me. When I called Ray's phone again a month later the number belonged to someone else. I smothered my hope of seeing him ever again by imposing common sense on myself, telling myself that all those stunts had been fun but not that big of a deal, and neither had those little therapy sessions we did, which I'd never mentioned to anyone, and don't think Ray ever did either. I held on to the dream transcripts though, out of sentimentality, I suppose.

I couldn't see any good reason why he had abandoned me like that. It was nice that he'd opened up and let me help him that way, but he never acknowledged how close we got. I couldn't believe that even as just good friends, after sacrificing all that time for him, even if he wasn't coming back and wouldn't be returning the favor of being there for me like I was there for him, he could've at least stayed in touch during my last year at school. Just hearing from him a few times would've been a huge help.

Instead, I studied alone like a fiend, trying not to drink too much, slowly bending my GPA back into better shape. I put off the applications for grad school, financial aid, and grants. I just didn't have the energy anymore. Though my grades had suffered, I still graduated in the spring of 2002, without any honors but right on schedule in four years with my relieved parents smiling at me and cheering when some dean called my name.

Ten years later, I was in an elevator two thousand miles west of the city where Ray and I went to college and while I can't be completely sure, the music in there sounded very much like Muddy Waters' 'Mannish Boy' adapted for twelve-string guitar, a soft instrumental version with these nice, almost inaudible microtones. I stayed on the elevator to listen for a few more minutes smiling at people who probably thought I'd lost it.

Hearing that music was for me the second surprise I had since college that some part of Ray was still alive out there. The first came when I read online about a couple productions of *Dynamo Blues*, Ray's award-winning college play that triggered the crisis I helped him through. There had been a production in Savannah in 2005 and another in Oakland a few years later. It was cool to see his name on my computer screen under the words 'Written by.' I felt as if there were an invisible co-credit beneath it for me, like I imagine parents feel when their kids accomplish things.

I'm glad one of us had some artistic success. Mine probably would've been academic. Not that I haven't done pretty well—I make decent money. After college, my uncle offered me an entry-level gig doing human resources administration. It sounded boring, but I took it because it paid well. Now I've really chipped away at my school debt, and was able to move out west. I never made it to grad school. It just felt crazy to consider taking on more debt to go get, of all things, a Ph.D. in German literature. If the people in the program sucked, it was just going to be lonely all over again and twice as expensive.

I've never tried to get in touch with Ray and he's never reached out to me. I did almost contact his dad once. I'd been drinking bourbon after reading the transcript about Ray's dad and dead mom in that theatre; I still have well-preserved copies of all seven of the dream transcripts we created. It was after midnight and at the kitchen table I was ready to send an email to Ray's dad at the Peabody in Baltimore, when I realised I'd never met the man. I froze and got the feeling I was about to write to the other world, not because the guy was rich, more like a ghost, since I only knew him through Ray's dreams and comments years ago about how badly they used to get along. Maybe Ray's dad hadn't spoken to him in years either. I had enough sense that night to delete the email.

It's a bit embarrassing to still read the transcripts occasionally and get stuck thinking about college days. In my peaceful moments I can see that the transcripts are real evidence that I helped nurture Ray's talents, even if I didn't manage to accomplish the kind of things he did. I helped him. I thought of him and wanted him to succeed, maybe because I felt like I owed him for inspiring me, even if our friendship didn't turn out the way I hoped.

When I read the transcripts I remember sitting close to him and how sick but strong his face looked that day he whispered about his mom dying in that war when he was so young. I know that for him the dreams he told me held a meaning about her and death that he couldn't admit. He seemed to like how impossible it was. I got the sense, and still feel grateful to him for showing me, that he believed his fate would change for the better if he could figure out some small part of that secret's nature. For me, it was significant to see that even as brilliant as he was there were limits to what he could understand about himself and her.

He needed to reach out to the dead in his own way back then. Lately, it's started to make a lot of sense for me to think of Ray as if he were dead, too. I just sat down with coffee in the living room one Saturday morning, took a sip, looked around and thought that it would be nicer if I could imagine that Ray was just gone forever. It was as if I could see the words and finally feel them: you will never get Ray back. You will never find him again because there is no one like that for you to find. I could take those memories and do what feels natural, move him in my mind among the dead. He would belong to another realm for me, where my dad is now, and a cousin, an ex-girlfriend, and my grandmother. That's where Ray really belongs, after all, after so many years without any contact. If I could kill him off, I could maybe use him the same way he used his mom. My memory of his life connected to hers connected to mine would vanish, breaking the chain of caring so much and worrying about it, if possible, leaving me with my own life again. He wouldn't have to be a real person anymore, just a story emptying itself of memories about someone I may have loved, but who didn't have time for me because he was too preoccupied with things I never really understood.

I haven't been able to kill Ray off completely yet, but I did his memory some real damage in my mind the other night. I was lying on my couch reading the seventh dream transcript and halfway through I imagined Ray started to talk, warning me about my habit of looking back and reliving his old dreams so often. He was finally trying to be helpful, invoking the tale of Lot's wife, whispering about cursed people turning to salt and losing their souls. I imagined holding up the stapled transcript of his dream in my hands and tearing the pages in half from top to bottom. Holding the halves lightly in my hands, they would tilt and sway, letting the sentences I had typed slip off the pages, silencing Ray, forming a pile of small black letters on my chest. I could sit up on the couch and brush off his words. I would be free to forget him if I could stay strong. The only remnant of Ray would be a few torn sheets of blank paper twitching in my hands as I carried them toward the trash and steadied myself before throwing them away for good.

Appetite for Depletion
Thoughts on Michel Houellebecq by Rob Doyle

Let us be clear: Michel Houellebecq wants to bring you down. If you are happy in your life, he wants to spoil it. Not out of particularly noble motivations: his agenda is propelled by spite, hostility, resentment. He is a nihilist—not in the pure, passive sense (if that were the case, we would never have heard from him) but actively, virulently. He is engaged with the world to the extent that he wants to undermine it. He is not on the side of 'good' or of improvement, or of humanity. He is wretched and he wants to infect you—and all the West—with his misery. Because he happens to possess a genius for literary seduction and an authentically harrowing vision, there is every danger that he will succeed. This, to my mind, is what makes him the most fascinating of living novelists.

•

Objectively speaking, Michel Houellebecq probably should not be read. (I say that as an enthralled reader of everything he has ever published.) In a more robust, self-assured civilisation, Houellebecq and his ideas would be firmly suppressed, or he would simply be ignored by an indifferent public. Houellebecq knows this; the fact that he exists is part of his indictment. His success is his accusation.

•

Houellebecq drains all the cheer out of life, because cheer requires illusion, ignorance and hypocrisy—all of which are healthy traits in any virile psychic economy, as Nietzsche understood. Again, Houellebecq knows this, having read his Nietzsche. But Houellebecq refuses us our vital errors, driven as he is by (more or less conscious) malice and resentment. In a sense, I wish I had never read him; though of course this is not really true—I read him raptly, and he inflicted exactly the kind of wound I was longing for.

After Nietzsche had first read Schopenhauer, his friends said he was no longer the man he had once been, so enervated was he by his predecessor's overwhelming pessimism. It took Nietzsche many years to claw his way back, to overcome Schopenhauer and posit new, anti-Schopenhauerian values. It would take a formidable force of will to overcome Houellebecq, once you have allowed him to whisper his insinuations in your ear. It may even be that, if you do have ears for Houellebecq, then you are already beyond help.

•

Houellebecq stands apart from other literary nihilists like Thomas Bernhard, the Marquis de Sade, Bret Easton Ellis, and H.P. Lovecraft (the subject of Houellebecq's first book), in that his vision—entropic, pitiless, terrible—strives for, and arguably achieves, objectivity. He has done his research: Houellebecq's nihilism, which he intends to be viral and global, has the unholy force of a cold and rigorous analysis, an unflinching depiction of a species and a civilisation in terminal drift. He is one of the few authors who I would describe as terrifying. Driven by rage, armed with the scientific method, and fine-tuned to the feel of the age, the despicable Houellebecq recreates our world in a harsh glare of empirical veracity, so that we are forced to see how loveless, hopeless, and brutal it has become.

A Bernhard, or even a Martin Amis, provokes or upsets us through a spewing forth of their private horror, their subjective, pathological, or paranoid conviction that all is putrid and hostile. Ultimately, though, someone like Bernhard comes to seem a bit silly. Close his book, pour a glass of rum, chat with your friends, and you will soon be persuaded that the world according to Bernhard, though unpleasant and claustrophobic, can be left safely outside the door; it is only the twisted vision of one unhappy man, an Austrian maniac of little relevance to your life. His interminable, denunciatory rants, though entertaining and sometimes unsettling, are at bottom as uninformed as the morbid pronouncements of a teenage Slipknot fan. (Judged solely on the depth and originality of his thought, Bernhard is an essentially adolescent writer.) Bernhard's life-hate and heavy-metal disgust for humanity are sincere and pure, but finally not very interesting, because they never reach beyond themselves, beyond Thomas Bernhard. They remain local, recognisably the subjective afflictions of the author and his interchangeable, misanthropic, neurotic characters. This despite Bernhard's attempts to universalise the tenets of his life-hate, most frequently through a spurious but catchy application of the collective first-person pronoun. The subversive effect of Bernhard's torrential prose, spewed out in book after scarcely distinguishable book, is limited by the banality of his thought, which can be summed up in a few short sentences: life is awful; humanity is ridiculous; go and kill yourself. Bernhard cannot finally undermine us as he would like to. We cannot take him seriously enough to feel genuinely threatened. We close his books and get on with our lives.

Not so with Houellebecq. He is more dangerous, because he is more interesting, and he has read more. Equally hostile and aggressive as Bernhard, Houellebecq has gone much further: he has amassed the intellectual firepower to back up his assault on the very foundations of healthy, unconflicted life. His terroristic motive is subjective, forged in a biography replete with bullying, exclusion, and the agony of being unloved (his 'old slut of a mother' comes in for a lot of blame), but the vision he inflicts is terrible and insidious because it claims to represent the world as it is in itself—adrift, exhausted, at the bitter end of the Western Enlightenment project, and stripped of the last vestigial enchantments.

Backed up by a deep reading in sociology, anthropology, evolutionary biology, and philosophy, Houellebecq's intention is to perpetrate your undoing on an objective, incontestable basis. He wants to close off every air vent, block every fissure through which the oxygen might get in; he wants to smother all possibility of illusion.

•

The facts of life according to Michel Houellebecq (a sampler):

– God is dead, of course; and with him went purpose, order and hope. The time for getting worked up about all that has passed. (Not the heroic, but the mundane stage of atheism.) The primary fact of a godless cosmos will simply be assumed: our intention will be to pursue the *implications* of this primary fact in a more rigorous and merciless manner than almost anyone has done since Nietzsche (who lost his nerve in the end), particularly as it applies to human sexuality. You will get hurt in the process. We offer no apology; we too are hurting.

– Europe is dying. The rot has set in, and the process is irreversible. The grand dreams of expansion and utopia have ended. We inherit an abandoned project, for which we no longer have the conviction, the discipline, or the backbone. Lacking any higher motivation, we fall back on ourselves, living shallow, aimless lives dedicated to the gratification of desire; these lives add up to nothing, are worth nothing, and cannot save us from the humiliating decline of our bodies (now a meaningless process), and lonely, hopeless deaths. 'That is your fate,' as the refrain runs through a certain Buddhist sutra. 'You will not escape it.'

– We are all obsessed with getting older, and we have good reason to be. Devoid of an overarching mythical, religious, or even political narrative, our civilisation worships youth and despises the old. To be young is the sole desirable condition: the young can give and receive pleasure, and they are attractive. These are the only possible remaining values (a late consequence of our civilisation's materialist suppositions.) Indeed, the bodies of the young are 'the only desirable commodity this world has ever produced.' In a universe bereft of illusions, sex is the single goal worth pursuing, the only experience which needs no justification beyond itself. Get it while you can.

– Our purported taste for egalitarianism in all things is revealed for what it is—shallow and inadequate—when we cast a cold, philosophic-anthropological eye on the arena of sexuality. There, we realise that inequality is inherent to life itself, that domination and submission, superiority and inferiority, are stubborn, bitter facts that will forever undermine any ideological attempts to pretend they don't exist. In a civilisation that bends over backwards to assure us all of our racial, social, political, and gender equality, we cannot help noticing that, when it comes to sex, some animals are more equal than others. Born into an arbitrary and vicious caste-system of attractiveness and ugliness, some live blessed lives of sexual plenty, while others are untouchable.

Sexual inequality has always been around, of course, and would not have become a source of newfound agony, had the kind of sexual morality that, ironically, persists today only in staunchly Islamic, Christian, or otherwise pre-modern societies, held fast. But the sixties came along and fucked it all up—suddenly anyone could screw anyone else; the fragile bonds of projection and fantasy needed to foster deep, life-long relationships took a battering, and love was seen for the first time to shit itself in fear. The bulwarks dissolved: man found himself, naked and shivering, in the merciless glare of the sexual free-market. Thus began *the extension of the domain of the struggle*.

•

The end of the nineteenth century gave us the Antichrist, Friedrich Nietzsche. A century later, we behold the Anti-Nietzsche[1], Michel Houellebecq. Houellebecq is Nietzsche stripped of hope, vigour, nobility and grandeur. For Houellebecq, man is not something that must be overcome, but at best domesticated, ideally put out of its misery. Nietzsche's gravest nightmare was the spectre of the 'last man': democratised, feminised, socialist, contented, slovenly, timid; a herd creature, a couch potato, a pen-pusher. Nietzsche (growing desperate) declared with increasing shrillness that the superman would come, that he *must* come, to enslave or exterminate the 'last man' and inaugurate a heroic new age of cruelty, grandeur, and cheerfulness. Having uttered his prophecies, Nietzsche raged, danced and ranted right into the madhouse, and the brink of the twentieth century. A couple of apocalyptic wars and a sexual revolution later, Houellebecq turned up to announce, with a jaded shrug, that the superman would not, in fact, be coming. Nothing would come. The time for great hopes had passed. All we had now was the global shopping centre ('the only horizon'), and we might even be glad of it. Our only remaining access to transcendence lay in the nerve endings along our cocks and clitorises. 'I am the last man,' said Michel Houellebecq,

---

1 The phrase is taken from Malcolm Bull's provocative essay, 'Where is the Anti-Nietzsche?' (*New Left Review 3*, May-June 2000)

and blinked. 'Now leave me alone with my Phuket whore and my modest vices, so I can while away my pointless life. Don't talk of effort or heroism, or the wicked laughter of Dionysus that will ring out across the earth. It will not. Just be quiet. If the tedium of your existence is relieved by a nice blowjob now and then, and there is an efficient police force at hand to keep you safe from thugs and Arabs, count yourself lucky. Don't neglect to avail of Third World sex tourism, if you can afford it and are ugly enough to need it. That will take the edge off. Everyone's a winner. Less talk of upheaval, progress, and the grand destiny. Stop your bloody nonsense. Be quiet. Better.'

As the Anti-Nietzsche, Houellebecq places himself beyond Nietzschean accusations of unacknowledged *ressentiment* simply by being wholly truthful, to the point of comic self-abasement, about his own status and motives: he *is* resentful; he *knows* himself to be inferior; he *will* use his spleen and cunning to diminish his hated betters. And why shouldn't he? After all, life is bitter and meaningless, and Houellebecq is abject, with nothing to lose—why not exert the modicum of power he has, just for the hell of it? Houellebecq's agenda, then, differs from that of the Christians, anarchists, democrats and socialists who Nietzsche despised, in that Houellebecq is never deluded about what drives him. He is beyond reproof, because he is beyond redemption. This is an infuriating, irresponsible, dangerous position, the literary-ideological equivalent of a suicide bombing. Houellebecq is going out, and his only concern is that he takes as many of us with him as he can.

•

Houellebecq is brutal, as brutal as a writer can be without being utterly repugnant. Yet his brutality is complicated because he himself tends to be on its receiving end (and not only in the most obvious case, in which the character 'Michel Houellebecq' in *The Map and the Territory*, is eviscerated and decapitated by a psychopathic avant-garde artist.) Houellebecq is among the wretched, the shamed, the contemptible, but he responds to his downtrodden status not with a Christ-like love for his fellow sufferers, or a revolutionary inversion of values, but with a resigned, masochistically rigorous elucidation of his abjection. His motto might be: *to disturb the comfortable, and finish off the disturbed.*

And yet Houellebecq's very brutality finally transpires to be a sort of compassion. The truths presented in blunt, unadorned prose throughout his novels are precisely those that are almost never uttered in our society, not even in literature, because they are too shameful and too deflating to bear. For instance: some people are unattractive, and therefore receive no love, nor even the relief of sexual gratification. Such people often feel themselves to be worthless and better-off dead, and in some instances they may be correct: today there is no viable myth of consolation, Christian or otherwise, to blunt the agony of horrible lives—last will not be first, and the meek will inherit nothing.

Merely to say such a thing is to be brutal; there is no way to say it *without* being brutal. But which is more brutal: to say it, or to remain silent on the matter, which remains excruciatingly true? Which is more compassionate?

•

Along with his beat-up, underdog likeability, it is Houellebecq's sense of humour that preserves him from our outright hostility. Amid the nastiness, hardcore sex, and depressing rhetoric of his books, there is plenty of whimsy, wit, and a grin-inducing eccentricity of style. And then there is a starker, more unsettling kind of anti-humour which feels distinctively Houellebecqian, grounded in unnerving bluntness and calmly acknowledged desperation. Consider this passage from *Platform*:

> As a wealthy European, I could obtain food and the services of women more cheaply in other countries; as a decadent European, conscious of my approaching death, and given over entirely to selfishness, I could see no reason to deprive myself of such things. I was aware, however, that such a situation was barely tenable, that people like me were incapable of ensuring the survival of a society. Perhaps, more simply, we were unworthy of life.

Nobody should speak of themselves in this way. The condemnation is severe, almost absolute ('perhaps… unworthy of life'), but the tone is casual to the point of drollery. Sometimes, comedy is achieved by simply speaking the truth in as clear and direct a manner as possible. At other times, what tickles us is the spectacle of a man, lucid and articulate, holding forth on his own hopelessness—our laughter is triggered by the intuition of a common fate. In Houellebecq's anti-humour, we find both strands running together, without interruption.

•

A further paradox: by way of a gleeful and brazen disrespect for literature, Houellebecq helps to keep literature respectable, and vital too. His novels are an odd, hybrid phenomenon: a kind of high-brow trash, an intellectual pulp-fiction. They are sleazy, punky, hyperbolic, and sometimes preposterous, yet always of an extreme seriousness. Houellebecq's insolence—the embodied insult and rebuke that is Michel Houellebecq—infuses even the form of his novels, which brashly announce themselves without concession to novelistic refinement or delicacy. At times, it really seems as if Houellebecq is deliberately doing all the things that are supposed to constitute 'bad writing'. His characters, often recruited to embody and promulgate the author's ideological prejudices, launch into improbable, lengthy speeches rather than carry out naturalistic dialogue; his narrators, be they in the first or the third person, do the same. Houellebecq's prose is thick with unabashed grandiloquence, and portentous utterances that even Martin Amis might blushingly cross out. (One chapter in *Atomised*, charting the love affair between two characters, actually begins, 'In the midst of the suicide of the West, it was clear that they had no chance.')

I like to think that Houellebecq's incessantly flaunted bad taste is a performative strategy intended to make the point that neither 'good taste,' nor literature itself in its more polite and respectable guises, have done much to avert our drift into disorder, depletion and meaninglessness. Literature, it is widely felt, is in danger of becoming a nostalgia, a museum-experience for hangers-on to a vanished past, of scant relevance to a stark and addled hypermodernity. Perhaps the only way for writing, for novels, for literature to connect with the new humans is to enact a vigorous, radicalised contempt for itself.

Having admired *Atomised*, Julian Barnes wrote a review of Houellebecq's subsequent book, *Platform*, highlighting all the ways in which it fails as a traditional novel—and thereby completely missed the point. For all his uncouthness as a novelist—deliberate or not—the one thing that Houellebecq will not do is write worthy, respectable, insipid stories that we forget as soon as we close the last page. For all its flaws, a book like *Platform* sears itself into the consciousness of many who read it; readers overlook its lapses as a traditional novel—its poor taste, sloppiness and indecorum—because of the electrifying sensation of encountering an author with something urgent and unheralded to say.

You can't really be an interesting novelist today, perhaps, if you have an uncomplicated faith in literature's undented relevance to contemporary humanity. Of course, every few years some David Shields comes along and tells us that the game is up for the novel; but this only happens because it's always true—novels have to continually reinvent themselves in order to stay fresh and relevant (stay novel) to human beings whose social, psychological, and technological landscapes are in constant morphosis. So far, despite every pronouncement of its demise, the novel has proven adaptable enough to stay relevant in the face of each cultural rupture since the dawn of the form in the seventeenth century. The world has always been changing, and for the most part the novel has kept the pace. But never has the world undergone such rapid and disorientating mutations as we have lived through in recent decades. A contemporary novel which relies on models created by the conditions of a vanished era, and which favours traditional novelistic themes over the weird matter of our post-human lives, runs a high risk of irrelevancy. Such a novel might be read, but perhaps only dutifully, and to little effect, by people who have internalised the idea that reading novels *is a good thing*, or nostalgically, by those to whom novel-reading is an act of defiance or an anxiety-suppressant amid a disorientating, post-literary techno-culture (I sometimes suspect myself of belonging to either category).

Ironically, Houellebecq claims to be influenced predominantly by nineteenth century authors (with a shot of science-fiction to spike up the concoction). Yet he understands, along with the more engaging of contemporary novelists such as the post-Nobel J.M. Coetzee and the late David Foster Wallace (a more pious analyst of our malaise than Houellebecq), that the mode of living in the 'literary' cultures of Europe and North America, at this late historical moment, is too estranged from that of our forebears for the old techniques to really hit home any more. As ever, a new kind of novel is needed to honour the singularity of our suffering and the foreignness of our struggle. Or, as Houellebecq wryly puts it, 'We're a long way from *Wuthering Heights*, to say the least.'

•

In *Public Enemies*, a book comprising the correspondence between Houellebecq and Bernhard-Henry Levy (which, incidentally, would be twice the book it is if they had cut out all of BHL's letters), Houellebecq recalls the shattering experience he had when first reading Pascal as an adolescent. 'It goes without saying,' he writes, 'that there must have been some *secret flaw* in me that I tumbled, feet together, offering not the least resistance, into the abyss that Pascal opened up beneath my feet.'

For me, reading Houellebecq for the first time exerted precisely such a ruinous fascination. I was twenty, studying philosophy, and locked into a three-year hell of severe depression and nervous derangement. Even though I knew I was badly disturbed (which is also how you know you are still sane), I had absolute confidence in the conclusions about the world, human life, and myself to which my relentless, pathological thought-processes had led me. Then I read Houellebecq, and the shock of recognition, like any perverse intoxication, was as gratifying as it was devastating. Houellebecq's vision spoke intimately and intensely to my own dismal worldview, while simultaneously compounding it, hounding out any residual hope, comfort, or vital illusion. Reading Houellebecq, I felt vindicated, yet even more alienated and suicidal than before. As Houellebecq himself understood with regard to his own epiphanic reading of Pascal, this was not a neutral reaction; there clearly pre-existed a receptivity to these kinds of truths, a masochistic need to be brutalised and tormented in just such a way. If I had been healthy, and not the feverish wreck I was then, I would have been immune to Houellebecq; I would, as so many do, have brushed him off as a preposterous French fad and a poseur.

By the end of that period, having somehow completed my studies, I realised that I needed to get away from Ireland. I decided to spend a year or two in Asia—not, like the characters in Houellebecq's books, to indulge in sex-tourism, but to deepen my engagement with meditation and Eastern philosophy, a source of clarity and replenishment during my struggle for psychic reintegration. Around this time, as I was saving money to leave Ireland, Houellebecq's fourth novel, *The Possibility of an Island*, was published in English. Still as fascinated by Houellebecq as I had ever been, I would pick up the novel in bookshops and pore over its cover (typically adorned with a nubile, bikini-clad blonde making fuck-me eyes). I would read and reread the blurb, then open the book and read random sentences. I was desperate to devour the whole thing. But I didn't; I put it back on the shelf and flew to Thailand having made the decision not to read it just yet, nor any time soon. I knew I might not survive it. If that is not evidence of an author's literary achievement and intensity, I do not know what is.

Since then, maturity and experience have mitigated the impact of Houellebecq's work on me—but only to a degree. I am no longer severely depressed, and so I am no longer inclined to consider Houellebecq's decimated vision the *whole truth*; but I still consider it an urgent and daunting aspect of the truth. I come back time and again to Houellebecq's books, always mesmerised, always aware that only a handful of authors can affect me so powerfully. But beyond that, Houellebecq has got under my skin; his eerie, impassive voice, which articulates such terrible things, never really goes away. Nor does what Houellebecq calls his 'bacterial' view of humanity—not a mere juvenile provocation, but a post-Christian, post-metaphysical insistence on seeing human beings and the cultures they engender in purely biological terms, with some strains acknowledged as being harmful and others beneficent. At times I feel as if Houellebecq has seduced me into theoretically cutting myself off from humanity, or cutting out my own heart.

There are two universal poles of attraction: one we can label replenishment, or spirit, or vitality, the other depletion, or decimation, or death. One offers sustenance, connectedness and direction; the other is the void. Life—at least, my life, but also, I suspect, human life—is a continuous negotiation with the two, a perilous effort to keep sight of the former (it becomes so vague, so boring), while forever succumbing to the lure—perverse, demonic, intense—of the latter. This struggle—between life and death as opposing objects of worship—has been around forever. But the parameters have now been altered. The void would seem to have the stronger arguments stacked on its side. The great question and challenge of our age—the supreme elephant in the room —is that of nihilism. Morality, justification, and purpose are no longer given to us; we are forced to choose, if not invent them. And if we are to be mercilessly clear-sighted and rational, knowing what we do now about the nature of things, then really, what is there that is worth committing to? What binds us, when all the ideologies and narratives are in ruin, and the illusions have been dispersed? Is there any compelling reason to climb out of the pit of self and seek connection to a greater truth and purpose? Do such truths or purposes even exist? The stakes are high. The struggle with nihilism is nothing less than the struggle to prevent the living soul, in all its fragility, contingency and miraculous beauty, from committing suicide. To arrive at a nihilist conclusion means the cutting of all links to a shared world, and a premature burial in the dead soil of solitary ego. Nietzsche saw this, and it broke his courage—he ended by summoning new gods, new illusions, thereby becoming, in Cioran's words, 'a false iconoclast,' 'an anti-Christian Christian.' Because of our epoch's objective, species-level uncertainty about what we are supposed to do with ourselves —what the future is for—it now takes only a mildly pessimistic bent or ontological curiosity to find oneself personally confronted with this crisis of nihilism. Some of us, for reasons of pathology or temperament, are intoxicated by nihilism's intense humming. We return to it as to a drug, or an abusive lover, or a charismatic tyrant. We keep coming back even as it batters, terrorises, and finally annihilates us. Residing at the furthermost pole of depletion, void, despair, and death, is Michel Houellebecq —the euthanasiast of hope and seducer to nothingness.

THE CITY by Stephen Crowe ©2013 www.invisibledot.net

Variations on a Theme
Adam Thirlwell interviewed by Susan Tomaselli

In the British literary establishment (and let's face it, named *Granta* Best Young Novelist not once but twice is 'establishment'), Adam Thirlwell is something of a Trojan horse: 'Good novelists (or, maybe more honestly, the novelists I like) are often not just avant-garde in terms of technique; they are morally avant-garde as well.' His novels—*Politics* (2003), *The Escape* (2009)—use Milan Kundera and Philip Roth as templates, and feature digressions on Osip Mandelstam, the Bauhaus and Saul Bellow, to name but a few. With their narratorial interventions and other unconventional stylistic quirks, they flaunt the usual rules of sexual comedies. But Thirlwell is a master of turning ideas upside down (and inside out), no more so than in his novella *Kapow!* (2012), a response to the Arab Spring that uses typography, fold-out pages and wordplay to mimic the noisy confusion of events as they emerged on Twitter and YouTube. It is the missing link between *Tristram Shandy* and the Mayakovsky's *For the Voice* as designed by Lissitzky. Thirlwell has always been interested in the international and the experimental, and his *Miss Herbert* (2007), named for an English governess who may or may not have been Flaubert's mistress, and may or may not have helped him translate *Madame Bovary*, is his brilliant understanding of the possibilities of translation through a miniature history of the novel (or, an 'anti-novel, with novelists as characters,' as he puts it). It's a theme he continues to explore in *Multiples* (2013), a 'project for multiplying novels in any language,' inspired, partly, by Augusto Monterroso.

•

ST Could you maybe frame *Multiples*? How did the project come about? What is an experiment in multiplying translation? And how does it relate to artists' multiples?

AT I suppose *Multiples* had a sort of giant theoretical cause in the background; and then many, much smaller practical ones. The giant theoretical cause was wanting to prove something or investigate something further that I'd written about before—a wish to prove that in some way it would be possible to reconcile style and translation (like trying to mate two different species to create some mythical beast). I'd thought maybe you could, if you just thought differently about them both, if you relaxed or enlarged their definitions. I began to think of a work as a set of instructions for future construction—as you mention below. But the more I thought about it the more I wondered that, if that were true, then the real conclusions necessary would be even wilder than I'd first imagined. I started thinking of experiments with third languages, and imitations rather than literal translations. But while theory is one thing, in the end the fun is the practical results. That was how I had a very vague utopian idea of a series of stories that would be translated by a series of novelists—to see what would happen to the story by its end: which would be partly an experiment with what we meant by an original, and translation, and also what we meant by style. There, however, I would have happily paused—just contemplating this imaginary experiment. And therefore the true cause of this project actually existing was the mistake of mentioning that very vague ideal to the novelist Vendela Vida, so that suddenly, weeks later, I was on Skype and agreeing to set up a giant version of this ideal for *McSweeney's Quarterly* in San Francisco—which in the end comprised twelve stories, each of which got translated and retranslated in series of up to five versions.

As for the title, that emerged as I tried to think about what it was we were creating, as the project began to grow. And I suppose *Multiples* was a deliberately double title. In that on the one hand it was a kind of joke, since these are almost the opposite of artists' multiples—these writers' multiples are each entirely different objects, they're reproductions that are all originals—and yet at the same time I wanted to imply that maybe there was a way of seeing these multiples as more similar to artists' multiples than might at first be obvious: that in some way each version, however zany it might seem in relation to the original, was still a flawless reproduction, too.

ST Beckett changed languages because he wanted to be 'ill equipped,' because French allowed him to write 'without style.' You've deliberately chosen novelists rather than translators because of their style, haven't you? How did you assemble the writers for the project?

AT (Don't you think though that Beckett's reasons he gave for writing in French aren't quite right? It seems to me that there's something about the usefulness of French for minute distinctions, that exhaustive clockwork of symmetric syntax, that's somehow linked to his discovery of his own exhaustive style… Anyway, sorry, that's a digression.)

Yes, I chose novelists and deliberately excluded translators—not because I have such a hatred of translators, but because I wanted to see what would happen to the style of the original when faced with people whose usual mode is to subject everything they see to their own style... I wanted to exaggerate the problems facing the story's survival.

And I assembled the writers in a zigzagging way—beginning with as many friends as possible, and then proceeding through friends of friends and then dream luminaries like J.M. Coetzee and Javier Marías. The deep project was: I wanted novelists, overall, who each possessed a particular style; and who in their different ways were engaged in the creation of a unique linguistic pattern. But, as in every composition, the initial freedom was constrained by the first moves in the sequence—so that I had to keep filing in the pattern formed by each novelist in the series: if a French novelist could translate from English, that meant I then needed to find an English novelist who could translate from French, and so on... And if there are more English-speaking novelists who can translate from Spanish than they can from, say, Chinese, that's why there are fewer Chinese novelists than Spanish-speaking ones.

ST Style is something you've discussed before. In *Miss Herbert* you said that style is not national and the style of a novel was a 'set of instructions...never able to create an entirely unique, irreplaceable object.' This is how translation is possible, isn't it? It's translation as a variation, rather than a precise reproduction. Thomas Bernhard wasn't a fan of translation: 'Translations hit the market as distortions /

It's the dilettantism / And the dirt of the translator / That makes a translation so repulsive.' But isn't that the point of *Multiples*? Distortions? After all, Paul Klee thought genius was an 'error' in the system; Bolaño that the sign of a work of art was to let it be translated, let the translator be far from brilliant.

AT I love that Bernhard quotation. And of course, he's right, in a way. That disgust is universal. The existence of any translation is a kind of disgrace. But also I think that, philosophically, he's deeply wrong. His disgust is just the obverse of a crazy dream, the dream of the perfect translation—which itself is based on a dream of a perfect style. But there's no such thing as the perfect style, which is why there's no need to be angry that no translation is perfect, either. A translation can only be an imitation in certain ways: it can never be comprehensive. Which is why distortions are, in the end, to be encouraged. For even the purest, most faithful translation will represent a systematic distortion. So that yes in the end, I'm with Bolaño: a work that resisted all translation wouldn't in fact be a work of art at all. A translation is a reading, an interruption. So my ideal with this project was to intensify that distortion: to create a multiple thing, all grainy and pollinated and drifting…

ST You've translated before, Nabokov's 'Mademoiselle O' for your book *Miss Herbert*. As Nabokov advocated literal translation, did the practice of translating him influence your translation? Did it cast a shadow over *Multiples*?

AT Definitely when I was translating 'Mademoiselle O' I tried to make a translation that Nabokov would have approved of…I made it as sternly as I could. But I think *Multiples* was my anti-Nabokov project. And it was partly prompted by discovering something I hadn't known before—when writing for the *NYRB* on Nabokov's translations. It turned out that Nabokov himself had made a very different sketch for a translation of *Eugene Onegin*—three stanzas—which instead of the stern literalism he advocated later were written in a lovely imitation of Pushkin's metre. I wish VN had continued with that translation! It would have been the perfect recreation of Pushkin in English. And it was the direct opposite of his later theories. And so it was thinking about the reasons for VN's shift in ideas about translation that made me wonder if in fact there could be another kind of ideal translation, too. *Multiples* is my revolution. Or self-coup.

ST Didn't you also translate Gogol, Chekov, Kundera, Hrabal, Schulz? And turn *Madame Bovary* down? Is translation something you may return to? Why don't novelists translate more?

AT It's true I made drafts of translations for *Miss Herbert*—as well as 'Mademoiselle O'—which included stories by all those novelists. And I decided in the end to put them aside. The reason for not translating *Madame Bovary* was a pure problem of time. It would take so many years to do it properly! Which is I think the main reason why novelists don't translate more. But also there's a cultural reason for that lack which I wanted to question with *Multiples*: I feel that prose gets treated with too much orthodoxy, as opposed to poetry. There's a tyranny of the idea of the professional. Whereas me, I want a prose version of Lowell's *Imitations*!

Whether I'll go back to translation, I don't know. For the moment I'm wondering if I've done what I want to do with translations… It was some necessary route of dismantling.

ST You've said that you've wanted to make translation more joyful. What has been the response to *Multiples* from translators? From its contributors?

AT Well, luckily, people seem to have liked it… I think its contributors all enjoyed the process—especially since it was often the first time they'd ever done a translation at all. And they were often surprised by the nature of the difficulties—which are always so minute and recalcitrant. So in fact maybe the contributors themselves had a harder time in the actual making of the texts… I think they were then kind of amazed, as was I, when they discovered how vast the finished project had become.

I did worry that translators in particular would be enraged by the exclusion of translators. But instead brilliant translators like Daniel Hahn and Maureen Freely and Frank Wynne all seem to like it. Which I'd hope they would, I suppose—as after all it's a project whose intent is purely benign, in one sense—to reveal translation as a possible form of art, and as a mode that demands more respect than it often receives. Although also it's true, it occurs to me, that this book does have its dark side. Perhaps an angry refusal of this project would also be rational. Because there's a way that this comic treat is also a noir contraption: like I've always liked those sinister objects by Man Ray, that are almost toys, but aren't. Its implications for what a translation could be, or what an original could be, or what is happening at all when a translation is being read, well I suppose it's true that they're quite malign…

ST *Multiples* is a visual treat, as was *Miss Herbert*, and *Kapow!* was described as a Cy Twombly painting with their cascading texts. Would you collaborate directly with an artist, is that something that interests you? Like the modernist little magazine collaborations, or more recently, László Krasznahorkai and Max Neumann, or Alexander Kluge and Gerhard Richter?

AT I love *Animalinside*, and what Kluge and Richter have done too. And I've always adored those multimedia modernist magazines: or also the books in Moscow in the 1920s, like El Lissitzky's Mayakovsky. So yes, the idea does interest me. And I do like producing books that have some kind of visual kink to them. (Even if, in the case of *Miss Herbert* and *Multiples*, that was really the contribution of the publishers and their designers, rather than a deliberate part of the work's thinking.) And I do also sometimes feel sad that a certain freedom of thinking about art among artists isn't quite replicated in the thinking about literature. I enjoy trying to imagine ways in which literature could be made more liberated—one of which, definitely, would be collaborations with artists themselves. I think I also find the general idea of collaboration intriguing—and partly as a result of this giant project. It's interesting how far literature is conceived as a singular project: whereas it seems to me that there are more mini collectives and collaborations that are possible. Not just artists and writers, but also writers together: like Bioy Casares and Borges inventing their authors and works.

ST What can you tell us about *Lurid & Cute*? Is that finished? What's next for you?

AT It's a novel. Oh, what can I tell you? I'm trying to invent the most innocent narrator in world literature, who the reader gradually realises is also the most frightening… That's the ideal. But it isn't finished. Not at all. Finishing it is what's next for me. I hope.

Vagues
Joanna Walsh

There are many people in the oyster restaurant and they all have different relations to each other, warranting small adjustments: they ask each other courteously whether they wouldn't prefer to sit in places in which they are not sitting, but in which the others would prefer them to sit. Sometimes entire parties get up and the suggested adjustments are made; sometimes they only half get up then sit down again, and they are not. Some of the tables in the restaurant face the beach and have high stools along one side so that diners can see the sea. Others have high stools on both sides so that some diners face the sea and others, the restaurant, but both, each other's faces. Because of the angle of the sun and

Прошлым летом на море
Перевод Анны Асланян

В прибрежном ресторане, где подают устриц, много людей, всех их связывают друг с другом разные взаимоотношения, которые требуют внесения небольших поправок: беседующие вежливо предлагают друг другу пересесть в тех случаях, когда выбор одних не соответствует предпочтениям других, с тем чтобы достичь искомого соответствия. Иногда со своих мест поднимаются целые компании, и соответствия удается достичь; иногда они лишь приподнимаются, и достичь его не удается. У некоторых столиков в ресторане – тех, что ближе к воде, – стоят высокие стулья, причем с одной стороны, так что посетители сидят лицом к

of the straw shades over the tables, the people who face the sea are also more likely to be in the shade. Not everyone can face the sea, not everyone can be in the shade.

The waitress passes. The people who face the sea cannot see her and cannot signal to her with their eyes. Facing the sea they can signal to nothing, as nothing on the beach can receive their signals, not the seagulls nor the mother and toddler who are too far away, nor the occasional stork that picks through the rubbish. Yes, the beach has rubbish, though not much, and though the restaurant, by its presence, makes the rubbish unmentionable. All the beaches along this coast have some rubbish: either more, or less than this beach. Here in the restaurant the diners who face the sea may notice it or ignore it, but they must accept the rubbish as part of the environment,

морю. У некоторых столиков высокие стулья стоят с обеих сторон, так что одни посетители сидят лицом к морю, а другие – к залу ресторана, причем и те, и другие сидят лицом друг к другу. Угол падения солнечных лучей и угол наклона соломенных зонтиков над столиками таковы, что у посетителей, сидящих лицом к морю, больше шансов оказаться в тени. Не все имеют возможность сидеть лицом к морю, не все имеют возможность оказаться в тени.

По залу проходит официантка. Люди, сидящие лицом к морю, ее не видят и не могут подавать ей знаки глазами. Они сидят лицом к морю, а следовательно, подавать знаки им некому, поскольку некому на эти знаки откликнуться: ни чайки, ни мать с маленьким ребенком, находящиеся слишком далеко, откликнуться не могут, как не может откликнуться и аист, время от времени прилетающий сюда порыться в мусоре. Да, на пляже есть мусор, которого, впрочем, немного и о котором, впрочем, само приcутствие ресторана заставляет забыть. На всех пляжах этого побережья есть мусор: на

just as they must accept the seaweed that covers the stones near the sea with a green slippery layer and which although, unlike the rubbish, is naturally part of the environment, smells.

The smell of the seaweed must be accepted as part of the natural environment although it masks the scent of the oysters served at the bar, the smell of which is so similar but nevertheless, different enough.

Further along the beach, where the mother and toddler are paddling, the seaweed forms stripes of green which are more pleasing, though this may be the effect of distance. The mother and toddler could have picked a better beach. Although all the beaches along this shore have some rubbish, some have less seaweed, and fewer stones. This beach is not good for paddling, but perhaps it is good for oysters. Yes, the

одних больше, чем на этом, на других меньше. Здесь, в ресторане, посетители, сидящие лицом к морю, могут его замечать, а могут игнорировать, но так или иначе, они должны мириться с мусором, составляющим часть окружающей среды, как должны мириться и с водорослями, покрывающими камни у моря зеленым склизким налетом, которые, пусть и составляют часть среды – естественную, в отличие от мусора, – при этом распространяют вокруг запах.

С запахом водорослей, составляющим часть окружающей среды, следует мириться, пусть он и перебивает запах устриц, которых подают за стойкой, пахнущих очень похоже, но все же достаточно своеобразно.

В отдалении, в той части пляжа, где купаются мать с ребенком, водоросли образуют полосы зелени, которые производят впечатление более приятное, пусть этот эффект и объясняется расстоянием. Мать с ребенком могли бы найти пляж и получше. Мусор есть на всех пляжах этого побережья, однако на некоторых

seaweed, the rubbish, the smell, the stones must all be part of the environment oysters prefer, which must be the reason the oyster restaurant is here, allowing the customers, seated at the tables, to look out at the beach and the sea and, looking, to understand that it must be the environment natural to oysters, and to approve.

Because he has chosen to sit at a table looking out at the sea, in order to see and approve the environment natural to oysters including the seaweed the rubbish the seagulls the stork the stones the mother and the toddler, he cannot signal to the waitress and it is because of this, or because she is insufficiently attentive, or because the oyster bar employs insufficient staff during the busy summer season, that the waitress does not arrive with his order.

меньше водорослей, меньше камней. Этот пляж не создан для купания, зато он, быть может, создан для устриц. Да, водоросли, мусор, запах, камни – все это, вероятно, составляет часть благоприятной для устриц среды, а последняя, вероятно, и есть причина, почему тут имеется ресторан, где подают устриц, в котором посетители могут, сидя за столиками, глядеть на пляж и море, а глядя на них, понимать, что это, вероятно, и есть та среда, часть которой составляют устрицы, и радоваться ее присутствию.

Он решил сесть за столик, стоящий ближе к воде, чтобы видеть благоприятную для устриц среду, куда входят водоросли, мусор, чайки, аист, камни, мать и ребенок, и радоваться ее присутствию, а следовательно, не может подать знак официантке; поэтому, или потому что она недостаточно внимательна, или потому что владельцы ресторана в оживленные летние месяцы нанимают недостаточное количество персонала, официантка не приносит ему заказ.

He says: 'Maybe they will bring the entire order at once, though I would have thought they would bring the drinks first.'

He says: 'They do not have enough staff.'

They employ the number of staff they can afford to employ and serve at a pace at which the staff are capable of serving. The capacity is natural and proportionally correct. Il faut attendre.

He says: 'They have too many tables.'

We must also consider the number of staff the restaurant can afford to retain over the winter months, which we hope may remain steady al-

Он говорит: "Может, они принесут все сразу, хотя, казалось бы, сначала должны принести напитки".

Он говорит: "У них не хватает персонала".

Они нанимают персонал в таком количестве, в каком могут позволить себе нанимать, и работают с такой скоростью, с какой способен работать персонал. Пропускная способность ресторана подчиняется закономерным соотношениям. Il faut attendre.[1]

Он говорит: "У них слишком много столиков".

Рассмотрим также количество персонала, которое владельцы могут позволить себе нанимать, и его зависимость от времени года: это количество, по нашей гипотезе, остается постоянным и

though the population of the island must shrink by—what?—fifty—what? seventy—percent—and during which the catch of oysters may remain the same or may, unfairly, increase because the winter months are more likely to contain the letter 'r' during which it is said oysters are best eaten, as during their spawning season, which is typically the months not containing the letter 'r', they become fatty, watery, soft, and less flavourful instead of having the more desirable lean, firm texture and bright seafood flavour of those harvested in cooler, non-spawning months so, although all the tables in the restaurant will not be filled during those winter months in which the population of the island shrinks by—what?—forty-five—what?—eighty percent—we may hope that the number of serving staff employed by the restaurant will remain steady.

в зимние месяцы, хотя население острова, вероятно, уменьшается (процентов на пятьдесят? на семьдесят?), тогда как улов устриц может в эти месяцы оставаться постоянным, а может, вопреки справедливости, расти, поскольку в названии зимних месяцев с большей вероятностью содержится буква "р", а устриц, говорят, лучше всего есть именно в эти месяцы, поскольку в месяцы, когда они размножаются, а это, как правило, те месяцы, в названии которых буква "р" не содержится, они становятся жирными, водянистыми, мягкими, теряют вкусовые качества, лишаясь желаемых легкости, упругости и превосходных вкусовых качеств, свойственных тем устрицам, которых ловят в месяцы более прохладные, не предполагающие размножения, и тем самым, хотя в эти зимние месяцы, когда население острова уменьшается (процентов на сорок пять? на восемьдесят?), часть столиков в ресторане пустует, количество нанимаемого владельцами обслуживающего персонала, по нашей гипотезе, остается постоянным.

Theories:
* *During the off-months for the visitors, which are the on-months for the oysters, are the oysters packed in ice or tinned, and shipped to Paris?*
* *During the off-months for the visitors, which are the on-months for the oysters, do the serving staff shuck shells?,*

Or:
* *During the off-months for the visitors, which are the on-months for the oysters, are the restaurant, and the oysters, abandoned, and the staff laid off?*

Предположения:
* *Верно ли, что в месяцы, неблагоприятные для посетителей, которые одновременно являются благоприятными для устриц, устриц упаковывают в контейнеры со льдом или консервируют, а затем отправляют в Париж?*
* *Верно ли, что в месяцы, неблагоприятные для посетителей, которые одновременно являются благоприятными для устриц, обслуживающий персонал очищает устриц от раковин?*

Иначе:
*Верно ли, что в месяцы, неблагоприятные для посетителей, которые одновременно являются благоприятными для устриц, от ресторана, как и от устриц, приходится отказаться, а персонал, соответственно, уволить?

The waitress passes our table again. She does not stop.

He says: 'I think these are summer staff. They don't know what they're doing.'

In another country my husband may be sleeping with another woman. He may have decided, having the option, being for once in the same city as her, finally to sleep with the woman with whom I know he has considered sleeping, although he has not slept with her up to now. It is lunchtime. Where my husband is, it is not even lunchtime yet. If my husband sleeps with the woman he will do so in the evening. As he has not yet done so, as he has not yet even begun to travel to the city where she lives, to which he is obliged to

Официантка снова проходит мимо нашего столика. Она не останавливается.

Он говорит: "Наверное, это летний персонал. Работать не умеют".

Не исключено, что в другой стране мой муж спит с другой женщиной. Не исключено, что он, получив такую возможность, – в кои-то веки оказавшись с нею в одном городе, – решил наконец-то переспать с этой женщиной, возможность переспать с которой он, как мне известно, уже обдумывал, хотя до сих пор с ней не спал. Сейчас обеденное время. Там, где сейчас находится муж, обеденное время еще не наступило. Если он надумает переспать с этой женщиной, то произойдет это вечером. Это еще не произошло, он еще даже не выехал в город, где она живет, – куда он, независимо от того, надумает с ней переспать или нет, так или иначе обязан ехать по делам, – а я сижу здесь, в ресторане, где подают устриц,

travel for work whether he sleeps with her or no, and as I am here in the oyster restaurant at lunchtime in another country, there is nothing I can do to prevent this.

The man sitting opposite me, looking out at the sea the seaweed the rubbish the seagulls the stork the stones, all of which I cannot see but which I know are behind me, does not want to wait for his oysters any longer. He has come here to relax but the oysters are too relaxed for him. He says, 'Do you want to leave?' He half gets up as though about to leave but does not.

He wants to punish someone for the oysters' slow pace. He wants to punish the waitress, who has not brought his order, by leaving. As he is facing the sea, he cannot signal to the waitress, so he wants to punish me by leaving. He does

в обеденное время, в другой стране и, следовательно, помешать этому я заведомо не могу.

Мужчина, сидящий напротив меня, глядящий на море, водоросли, мусор, чаек, аиста, камни – на все эти вещи, которых я не вижу, хотя мне известно об их присутствии за спиной, – не хочет больше дожидаться заказанных устриц. Он приехал сюда, чтобы отдохнуть, но устрицы недотягивают до его представлений об отдыхе. Он говорит: "Хочешь, уйдем?" Он приподнимается, словно собираясь уйти, но не уходит.

Он хочет отыграться на ком-то за медлительность устриц; он хочет отыграться на официантке, которая не принесла заказ, то есть уйти. Сидя лицом к морю, он не может подать знак официантке, а следовательно, хочет отыграться на мне, то есть уйти, однако не уходит и потому хочет отыграться на ком-то (на официантке? на мне?), то есть не получить удовольствия от обеда.

not leave. Because he does not leave, he wants to punish someone (the waitress? me?) by failing to enjoy his lunch.

Already he has asked the waitress several things. In the queue for tables he asked the waitress for a table although he was not yet at the front of the queue. When he asked, he did not ask her but he said, *Excusez-moi*, which means, May I get through?, then he said, *Pardon!*, which means, I'm sorry!, then he made a noise that sounded French and indicated the tables with his hand. Then he said, *Oui? Oui?* which means, Yes? Yes? Then he asked me to ask the waitress for a table. I can speak French but, after the noise, I cannot.

Each time a group of people passed along the path by the restaurant, on bikes or on foot, he looked at them anxiously in case they were able to join the queue, but be

Он уже несколько раз что-то просил у официантки. Стоя в очереди, чтобы получить столик, он попросил у официантки столик, хотя очередь до него еще не дошла. Когда просил, он не обратился к ней с просьбой, а сказал: "Excusez-moi", что значит: "Разрешите пройти", потом: "Pardon?", что значит: "Простите?", потом издал звук, похожий на французский, и показал рукой на столики. Потом он спросил: "Oui? Oui?", что значит: "Да? Да?". Потом он попросил меня попросить у официантки столик. Я говорю по-французски, но после этого звука – увольте.

Всякий раз когда на дорожке у ресторана появлялась группа людей, на велосипедах или пешком, он смотрел на них с тревогой, боясь, как бы они не встали в очередь, а потом не ухитрились получить столик раньше него. В ресторане два входа, оба видны от двери, и он внимательно наблюдал за обоими, чтобы ни в коем случае не дать никому пройти без очереди. Оказавшись в очереди первым, он прежде времени рванулся к столику, но официантка не

seated at a table before him. There are two entrances to the restaurant, both of which are visible from the door, and he watched both carefully to make sure no one bypassed the queue. When he arrived at the front of the queue, he made a false start towards a table, but the waitress did not respond. He did not repeat this movement so as not to abandon his position at the front of the queue. He stood squarely at the front of the queue so that no one could pass until another waitress arrived to give him a table.

He has made an enemy of the first waitress. She will enjoy serving her enemy. Perhaps he too will enjoy this combat. I do not enjoy combat with waiters and waitresses although I am now, by association, also her enemy.

Now he is here, seated at the table that looks out at the

сделала ответного шага. Повторять это движение он не стал, чтобы не лишиться места первого в очереди. Он твердо стоял первым в очереди, чтобы не дать никому пройти, пока не пришла другая официантка и не провела его за столик.

Первая официантка записала его в неприятели. Ей понравится обслуживать неприятеля. Возможно, эта схватка понравится и ему. Мне схватки с официантами и официантками не нравятся, однако теперь она записала меня в его соучастники, а следовательно, тоже в неприятели.

Теперь он здесь, сидит за столиком, выходящим на море.

sea. It is the table he indicated, the table he desired, from which he can see the sea the beach the seagulls the stork the mother the stones the toddler the seaweed the rubbish and, at the other side of the table interrupting his view of all these things, me.

He says: 'I want to leave.'
He says: 'Do you want to leave?'
He gets up from the table.
He sits down at the table.

He stands up and walks from the table to the nearest door of the restaurant, during which time the waitress brings the drinks.

Though I am able in some part to share his anxiety about the table the drinks the oysters I find, because he is so angry,

Это тот столик, на который он указал, тот, за которым он пожелал сидеть, тот, откуда ему открываются море, пляж, чайки, аист, мать, камни, ребенок, водоросли, мусор, а визави – предмет, загораживающий ему вид на все эти вещи, то есть я.

Он говорит: "Лучше уйти".
Он говорит: "Хочешь, уйдем?"
Он поднимается из-за столика.
Он садится за столик.

Он встает и идет от столика к ближайшей двери, а официантка в это время приносит напитки.

Я отчасти разделяю его беспокойство по поводу столика, напитков, устриц, однако обнаруживаю, что, поскольку он вышел из себя, я эту задержку могу воспринимать ничуть не теряя хладнокровия.

Каждый столик сделан из распиленного ствола дерева, полукруглого в сечении, установленного на деревянных козлах.

that I can face their delay with complete equanimity.

The tables are each made from a semi-circular length of half the trunk of a tree set on wooden trestles. The high stools are of brightly-coloured powdered metal. Above the tables, the umbrellas of natural straw spell relaxation.

He is not keen to relax. He is keen to get on. He is already late for his next station of relaxation, for the beach, where we have an appointment to meet some friends of his at a strict hour. He is worrying that we will be late, that they will be anxious, that they, that he, will not be able to relax. He takes out his phone to check the time. We must be on time for the deckchair, the towel.

A speedboat drives directly at the restaurant from the sea, so

---

Высокие стулья сделаны из порошкового металла, выкрашенного в яркий цвет. Над столиками высятся, наводя на мысли об отдыхе, зонтики из настоящей соломы.

Отдых не вызывает в нем энтузиазма. Энтузиазм в нем вызывает продвижение вперед. Он уже опаздывает в следующее место запланированного отдыха, на пляж, где мы договорились встретиться с кем-то из его друзей в определенный час. Он волновался, что опоздает, что они будут беспокоиться, что у них – у него – не будет возможности отдохнуть. Он вынимает телефон, чтобы узнать время. Нельзя опаздывать туда, где ждет шезлонг, где ждет полотенце.

directly that I can see neither its sides nor any perspective, only its prow and the foam it generates. On its prow sit two people, a man and a woman, perfectly tan in black surf suits, and for a long time it looks like the boat will not stop and will continue to drive toward the restaurant arriving, unlike the people passing on the path on the other side of the restaurant by bike or on foot, through neither of the restaurant's doors but directly through the tables, bypassing the queue entirely.

He gets out his phone and checks the time again. About this time my husband must be leaving for the city in which the woman with whom he has been thinking of sleeping lives. As I know my husband is unlikely to tell me the truth about

В море появляется моторная лодка, идущая прямо на ресторан, настолько прямо, что в этом ракурсе мне не видно ее боков, вообще ничего не видно, только нос и пену, которая бурлит перед ним. На носу сидят двое, мужчина и женщина, покрытые ровным загаром, в черных костюмах для серфинга, и долгое время кажется, будто лодка не собирается останавливаться – так и будет приближаться к ресторану и в конце концов, в отличие от тех, кто появляется на дорожке по ту сторону от ресторана на велосипеде или пешком, попадет сюда не через одну из входных дверей, а прямо через террасу, вовсе избежав очереди.

Он вынимает телефон, чтобы снова узнать время. Примерно в это время мой муж, вероятно, собирается в город, где живет та женщина, с которой он подумывал переспать. Поскольку я знаю, что муж вряд ли скажет мне правду о том, переспал он с этой женщиной или нет, – хотя, возможно, надумает сказать мне, что

whether he sleeps with the woman or not—though he may choose either to tell me that he has, when he has not, or that he has not, when he has—I have taken the precaution of being here in the oyster restaurant with this man who may wish to sleep with me. As my husband knows that I know he is unlikely to tell me the truth about the woman with whom he will or will not have slept, so that, even if he tells me the truth, I will be unable to recognise whether or not he is being truthful, he must believe that if he sleeps with the woman, he will sleep with her entirely for his own pleasure. I, if I sleep with the man who is sitting opposite me at the restaurant, though I will not lie about whether I have slept with this man or not, will be unable to tell my husband anything he will accept as truthful, so must also,

переспал, не переспав, или что нет, переспав, – я в качестве меры предосторожности пришла сюда, в ресторан, где подают устриц, с этим мужчиной, который, возможно, захочет переспать со мной. Поскольку муж знает, что я знаю, что он вряд ли скажет мне правду о той женщине, с которой он то ли переспал, то ли нет, – так что, даже скажи он мне правду, я не смогу понять, верить ему или нет, – он, вероятно, считает, что если переспит с этой женщиной, то лишь для собственного удовольствия. Если я пересплю с мужчиной, который сидит напротив меня в ресторане, то пусть я и не буду лгать относительно того, спала я с ним или нет, муж не поверит ничему, что бы я ему ни сказала, а следовательно, и я непременно должна сделать так, что если я пересплю с этим мужчиной, то лишь для собственного удовольствия.

by consequence, make sure that, if I sleep with this man, it must be entirely for my own pleasure too.

The speedboat has turned and the people in it, revealed to be six in number, all uniformly and perfectly tan and black, are either on the boat or in the sea beside the boat and are, with no hurry, doing something or not doing something, perhaps mooring the boat so that they can come to the restaurant to eat oysters, or not mooring the boat but doing something else altogether.
 They are slim and tan and their slowness has kept them slimmer and tanner than the people who wish immediately to be in the restaurant eating oysters.

Моторная лодка повернула, и сидевшие в ней люди, числом, как обнаружилось, шесть человек, все равномерно покрытые идеальным загаром, обтянутые черным, теперь либо в лодке, либо в воде рядом с лодкой, все неторопливо чем-то занимаются или не занимаются, быть может, привязывают лодку к причалу, чтобы отправиться в ресторан есть устриц, или не привязывают лодку к причалу, а занимаются чем-то совершенно другим.
 Они стройные и загорелые, их медлительность помогает им оставаться более стройными и загорелыми, чем люди, которые желают немедленно оказаться в ресторане и есть устриц.

He says: 'Perhaps they are mooring and are coming to the restaurant to eat.'

At that moment, our oysters arrive and are eaten quickly.

All the time we have been at the restaurant there has been the sound of the waves quietly repeating. Vagues, I think, undulate: *on-du-ler*. The sound of the waves is pitched and modulated precisely so as not to intrude, distract, but so as to remain constantly audible. It is perfect.

Он говорит: "Может, они причалят и придут в ресторан обедать".

В этот момент нам приносят устриц, которые тут же оказываются съеденными.

Пока мы сидим в ресторане, все время слышится звук волн, тихий, повторяющийся. Vagues, думаю я, колышутся: on-du-ler.[2] Звук волн по высоте и тональности настроен безупречно: ни во что не вмешивается, не отвлекает, при этом его слышно постоянно. Идеальный звук.

---

1 Надо подождать (фр.)
2 Волны... колышутся (фр.)

crocodile
Colin Herd

I

under the cushion, beside the
cashew sweater, the sesame
trap. people, nearer the door!
nearer the breezes! and tucked-
in. visible, giddying, galois-toting

but nearer, on the enormous
buffet:

a so-so salad, nasturtiums,
onions and mini bales/
mozzarella sails.
10 herring roe roulades

like you said you said.

incredibly potent sorbets,
the sort that crack open
your jaw in spite of itself,
and clam it shut the same
poignant, almost

my kind of sheeting and towels
my kind of belts.
more shoes than you can swash
your buckle at in this walk-in
wardrobe next to the drive-through
off-license next to the pram.

people talk all the time and
want to be left. tongue for a
scaredy cat. tunes for a top.
bite me. which is to say it
does get pretty damn tempting
once in a while.

II

pique you're right. the blossoms
on the soles of his pumps!
the clay smears on his whites.
the grass less so, a vain and moody
cricketer. floppy pockets.

he didn't go in for all this unrelenting
pressure. when it seemed the opportune
minute, he'd pounce—ending the
misery. it's a facet's been noted
of me.

oh dear his difficulties breathing
and mine. his tact and menace.
he found me lounging around
those funny little padlocks
on the seine and i was
sizzled from that first glance
split open like a spud, sweating
like a superhero

a swoosh of my gaudy tail
which made a racket
he said i'll always have you
on my heart

III

driver. six iron. putter.
putter. 3 wood. seven iron.
putter. not bad. but this
hole has water on it, a
great expanse of muddy
duck egg plonk

i'm so growly because the
preppy trend's back

we'll get over-exposed
and nobody gives a button
(again!)

it's a look i associate with
modern hotel lobbies and
shopping centres

seductive sash cardigans,
paimio chairs designed for
tb patients, the fluid arms
flowing across the spectrum

of flicking, grimacing, frothing,

teething, distorting, seething,
scowling, sneering, convulsing,
agitating, until kingfisher
comes

they all disdain my elaborate
shows of intimidation

a furry wood head
cover taken off
& slung over the
clubs, making some kind
of point of it,

squeezing my jaws
together with the inside
of her leatherette glove and
my jealousies together with
the innards of her leatherette
glut

they do this thing called
synchronised driving

i've come to the epiphany
that the country club makes
me wild

IV
and not at home exactly but
comfortable enough in my
surroundings:

a frog in a bathtub, say
hopping all the way to the
rim

all those bubbles, salts,
sponges

and people, two of them,

splashing about and
making my journey so
awkward and painful,

bashing my delicate
little legs, which i
kiss myself to make them
feel better

so maybe not so tough
as all that but chipper
and resilient and free

V

obviously
the brackish smell takes me back
to my childhood. which in itself is
part of the
enjoyment.

swallowing the urge to snap,
i spent hours and hours everyday
just watching people's ankles

both feet off the ground for the
serve, and then back in view,
balancing on a balletic toe,
before shunting off in the
other direction

the
better the player the bigger the
thrill. it's mesmerising. and

all you can see is the shoes and
ankles.

you should try watching live tennis
your belly prodded with twigs
like, when i used to skulk around
the river bank, just next to the
courts

however much they convince
me that poplin check is the way to
go forward, i doubt they'll ever eradicate
my sock and trainer fascination

the rippling dimples of the grip

at one time i might have been a total
sucker for aertex. but i've been taught
since and have more sophisticated tastes

VI

measuring tape around
my neck, like a leash (which
i could chomp through
in 30 seconds flat but elect
not to)

him sitting there all smiles
on the dartboard shore,
his skin almost as crackled
as mine, from weeks and weeks
and weeks in biarritz, o-d-ing
on apricot kernel butter

him in the corridor watching,
her bedroom timpanist
pulling faces to try and

get me to smoulder

the photographer saying yes
he thinks they probably do
have a replacement just in case

VII

not some trite antidote for brand
amnesia
this is essentially a love story

what i will say is this:
yes i have had an advance
for this book already
and the next

they're remaking 'hook'
you want to know if it's true

they've photoshopped
my midriff a touch

when the leftist runs snare
on the pastry sector

more grotesquely slick and
when i'm re-emerging even
when i'm going into rehab,

floating, in my own right…

who wears the cologne
in our relationship?

who has the rights to syndicate
the cartoons?

you want to know when the resorts
whole luxury (or pretty much)
cars, parades, theme parks and
out into biscuit tins, soft toys,

you want to know if we'll end up
some sort of replacement
infantile monastery

scoops of baby and baby-sitter
crocs, to
identify with emotionally

somebody thought the public
needed a new figurehead, and
you think it's got something
to do with rené's death,
'giving me a voice, a personality'
to reinvigorate the brand

(serialisation in

le canard enchaîné
in book form
spilling my guts out

you want to know what marketing
genius came up with this plan

and you probably want to know
what i'm getting paid for it

VIII

peter saville redesigned me

redesigned me! me!
peter saville! me!

all he basically
came up with was a load
of tangled, squiggly lines

i took it as a compliment,
as you can imagine… after the
initial shock

and he says he
he knows so much
about those thoraxes

but more like what he'd look
like if i ever got hold of him
than what i look like

even on a bad scales day

in any case, i'm prepared to
let him have his day in the sun
basking in my reflected glamour

only problem would be if they
actually liked one of his designs
and wanted to adopt it
but that's unlikely

but i'll shuffle myself
undetectably under that bridge
when and if we come to it.

Various Assumptions
The Still Lives of the Artists by Kevin Breathnach

I write this essay every year and, every year, I see it morph to suit the quote that kicked it off a little better. 'Every artist's work changes when he dies,' says John Berger in his essay on Giacometti. 'And finally no one remembers what the work was like when he was alive.' This was never as I remembered it, never as I needed it to be. What I remembered Berger saying was that death changes not the *work* of every artist, but the *image*. Berger makes his claim immediately after some remarks on Giacometti's demeanour in a famous photograph showing him crossing the road in the rain, his coat pulled over his head for shelter. Berger says he looks 'like a monk,' but to me the photograph casts Giacometti closer to one of his own sculptures. It was an understandable slip of memory, in any case, and it caused no trouble in the end. I simply included the quote as I'd initially remembered it, and as usual nobody noticed. Still, I think there's something instructive about this particular misremembering. The work of John Berger had been changed, after all, and John Berger had not died. What I know *had* happened to him, however, might in some way account for his essay's curious reticence about the person who took the photograph in question. In 1994, about fifteen years before my memory experienced his work as somehow altered, John Berger had his portrait taken by Henri Cartier-Bresson. The occasion is described in *Photocopies*. Mid-conversation, the photographer turns away from Berger. Then quickly he returns. 'He has picked up his camera and is looking at what is around me again. This time he clicks.' For some photographers, collaboration with the sitter is of central importance; to Cartier-Bresson it was anathema. To be his subject was to feel one's subjectivity dissolve. It has now been ten years since he died. Isn't it odd? His work does not seem to have changed at all.

What are the defining characteristics of a Cartier-Bresson portrait? And to what extent do these characteristics make the work resistant to change? For one thing, there is the grey. His portraits are taken not in the reductionist style of Avedon, nor in the near-obscurity of Edward Steichen's blacked out oeuvre. These particular black-and-white photographs are shot in natural light, their unfurling shades of grey endowing their sitters with an air of nobility and thoughtfulness. 'Nothing was more important to him than respect for the various shades of grey,' says his biographer, Pierre Assouline. 'One day we will speak of CBG (Cartier-Bresson Grey) in the same tones as they speak of IKB (International Klein Blue).' Whereas the portraiture of Avedon and Steichen approaches, from opposing angles, a sort of photographic abstraction onto which the viewer is invited to project their own ideas, Cartier-Bresson's work is 'filled up' with the complex internal workings of a whole spectrum of monochrome. There is no space for the viewer to work with. No give. After leaving the developing room, his photographs develop no more.

Another portrait of Giacometti shows its subject from the waist up. It is a more traditional portrait; the sitter's face has been offered a good deal more autonomy this time. Giacometti stands to the right of the frame, his left-hand tucked neatly into his right inside-pocket. Caught in three-quarter profile, he seems to have emerged from the building behind him. He is a little dazed to find the texture of his newspaper so strongly echoed by what he remembers of his own face, the texture of which he knows is echoed by the door to his right, whose texture in turn will echo that of his jacket. Cartier-Bresson might as well have carved this tableau from a single block of stone. It is a closed-system of textural echoes made legible only by the subtle interaction of its various greys. It is evocative of touch, of fingertips, finally of sculpture. The portrait seems immovable. There is nothing to add, and no place to add it. It is as if, in truth, the building from which Giacometti has just emerged is none other than Cartier-Bresson's developing room.

The visual echo is by no means the sole preserve of texture or shade, however. In the geometrically precise work of Cartier-Bresson at least, it is detected most often in the transitory mirroring of certain shapes. So, for example, in his portrait of the surrealist writer and art critic, Michel Leiris, the subject is hunched down in the bottom left of the photograph, the rest of the frame given over to a bank of bookshelves in the sitter's personal library. Against one bookshelf there rests a ladder (already a resonant motif in the early history of photography) without which the books on the top shelf would be quite out of reach for this diminutive subject. Though the ladder is clearly consigned to the background, its central positioning occasions it to dominate our first glance at the photograph. Look at it for a moment, though, and the ladder is cast further back into the frame by a very pronounced vein zigzagging its way up Leiris' forehead, which at last becomes a sort of pictorial fulcrum. Not only does this visual echo delineate the photograph's field of depth; it also calls playful attention to both the contents of its subject's head (books) and the style of subject's books (cerebral). In Cartier-Bresson, the visual echo is suggestive of something slightly beyond the frame. It is always working to establish just enough context to let us imagine that we know something of the subject and their work. In the echo, there is allegory.

His photograph of Alexander Calder was taken in the sitter's home. Calder's face is large and plural. It dominates the frame. We might even say it has been granted the full pictorial autonomy befitting of such a large face were it not for the grid of vertical and horizontal beams cutting across the background in subtle evocation of the sitter's angular, architectural style of sculpture. Alone, the photograph recalls the work. But the manner in which it does so sounds an inter-photographic echo that speaks also of biography. In 1929, André Kertész made a portrait of Calder. The sculptor looks much younger now. His face is smaller, more singular. Probably he is handsome. It is difficult to tell for sure, though: his body has been obscured by the horizontal and vertical wires of the work-in-progress before him. Cartier-Bresson greatly admired Kertész. 'We all owe something to him,' he said, 'whatever we have done, Kertész did first.' He knew this photograph, he had studied it for a long time. He situated his own grid accordingly. Taken just six years before its subject's death, his portrait positions the architectural grid in such a way as to suggest that Calder's work has been fulfilled, that it is now *behind* him. Indeed, although Calder had two sculptures left in him, he spent most of the seventies painting luxury vehicles on commission. It would be some fifteen years before André Kertész would die. Yet his work was already changing. After Cartier-Bresson's portrait of Calder, the picture Kertész took no longer seems suggestive of anything but a lifetime's work to come. Now, the work stands *before* Calder, *only before him*. The image is smaller now, more singular. Probably it is handsome. It is difficult to tell. It has been obscured by the rhetoric of an image that has come to stand before it.

Cartier-Bresson liked to play with people's hair. His portrait of Roland Barthes shows the semiotician staring directly into the camera. His legs are crossed, though mostly cropped from the frame. With a cigarette in his left hand, Barthes leans his right arm back into his chair. His swagger is a little too studied. Behind him, an almost architectural row of files and folders strongly echoes the neat *en brosse* of his hair. Made in 1963, nearly twenty years before Barthes wrote his seminal work on photography, the picture's visual echo evokes the exactitude and the practice of categorisation so characteristic of its subject's early thought. The swagger would come more naturally in time.

He made his portrait of Susan Sontag a decade later. He had not tired of hair. The couch on which Sontag is seated takes up almost the entire frame, to which her sprawl is central. Her legs are also crossed (less cropped this time), while her hair is flecked with a grey well served by Cartier-Bresson's photographic palette. Unlike Barthes, her eyes avoid the camera's gaze. Her arms emerge from inside her coat, the sleeves of which fall regally from her shoulders, like a cape. The gathered cloth, bunched higher to the left than the right, echoes the shape of her hair perfectly. It is a stately, even sovereign, pose that appears doubled to evoke its subject's stately, even sovereign, prose. Within five years, Sontag will have written her own (and perhaps the very first) seminal work of photographic theory. ('In all this chaos,' she writes there, quoting Cartier-Bresson himself, 'there is order.') Right now, though, she is thinking mostly about film. In *Camera Lucida*, Barthes wrote that photography is tame if tempered by certain empirical or aesthetic habits such as leafing through a magazine in a hairdresser's. I bow to Barthes, but only to look beneath him. What I want to understand is the apparent sharpness of being photographed as if in a magazine *for* hairdressers that has stunned a certain few to reconsider the aesthetic habits of photography itself. The hair becomes the sitter: that is the *studium*. But did the sitter worry they'd become the hair? In any case, it is no surprise that Barbara Hepworth, whose unruly thicket is not so much echoed as *extended* by the plant life in the background, never composed her own treatise on photography. Her portrait is not one of Cartier-Bresson's best. Nothing is told about its subject except, perhaps, at a push, something about the negative space that Hepworth's sculptures lent meaning to. There is little meaning offered here. It probably needs a prop—one of the geometrically adventurous pieces from Hepworth's back catalogue, say, or even just a work-in-progress.

It was not unusual for him to draw on his subject's work in this way, especially in the case of visual artists. He gets Joan Miró standing before a number of his canvases wearing something of the same owlish expression as his painted figures. A bespectacled George Eisler is shown peeping over a self-portrait, as if appealing for his image to be considered only through his own art. In another full-body portrait of Giacometti, whom Cartier-Bresson must have photographed more than any other artist, the subject walks at three-quarter angle with a mid-sized sculpture held in both hands. His step falls in time to that of the towering *L'Homme qui marche I* to the left. 'After 1945 Giacometti's sculptures became thinner and thinner,' writes Berger. 'It was concluded that they were on the point of disappearing.' Here, his movements are so hurried that the film's exposure cannot (or chooses not to) keep up. His figure becomes blurred to the point where his outline appears every bit as indefinite as the sculptures. He is a ghost at last, a bridge between the living and the dead.

Avigdor Arikha is more assuredly present before the camera. In what is perhaps the most visually complex portrait in Cartier-Bresson's portfolio, the painter appears to the right of the frame. He turns his neck away from the painting. Now he is facing the camera. Upright he holds a painting which, slightly taller than he is, shows a standing female nude from behind. His left-arm stretches into the centre of the frame. The horizontal line it describes is echoed by a representation of the very same left-arm, which appears in a self-portrait propped on an easel occupying the bottom left of the frame. There, Arikha is represented standing in a pose so similar to the one he makes for Cartier-Bresson that it would appear to be emanating from a mirror were it not that the painted figure faces away from us. The mere suggestion of mirroring draws our attention back to the female nude. In the painting, we notice now, she is standing beside a mirror. She stands so close to it, in fact, that her reflection is largely obscured by her own body. Still, it is definitely there. Her legs, her pubic hair and her abdomen are all clearly visible. They constitute a reference that works within the larger context of the photograph to 'realise' its referent. It is as if this female nude, standing between Arikha and an enormous mirror, actually exists. Avigdor Arikha was a realist painter. He did not paint from memory or from imagination. He painted from life. 'Only this is true,' he said. With its realistically depicted figure depicted somehow realer still, it is tempting just to chalk it down as a skilfully made concession to its subject's art. It is quite a bit more than that, however. It is a self-portrait.

I'm not sure Cartier-Bresson would have agreed with Dorethea Lange's notion that every photo-portrait is a self-portrait. I don't believe he saw anything of himself in his portrait of Louis Aragon, for instance. I can't think he saw much of himself in his visions of Pound or Capote or Mauriac either. There are certain sitters, however, with whom he clearly identified. Their portraits speak to this. Like Cartier-Bresson, Arikha absorbed the lessons of his early artistic influence (Abstract Expressionism) before breaking out on his own to depict life as it was lived. It was not 'a return to figuration,' he said, but the figure had certainly returned. He understood texture and he understood geometry. He worked only in natural light and he finished a painting in one session. His artistic practice, grounded in immediacy, was spoken of as being directly analogous to Cartier-Bresson's *instant décisif*, that single moment when, the photographer believed, the world opened up and bared itself in flagrante. 'I prowled the

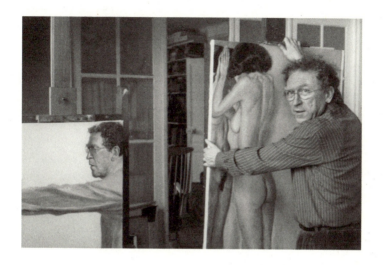

streets all day,' wrote Cartier-Bresson, 'determined to 'trap' life—to preserve life in the act of living.'

It is in this light that the portrait's internal logic starts to grind to its conclusion. The positioning of Arika's self-portrait invites the viewer to think of it not as a painting but as an image reflected in a mirror. The bottom left of the frame has become a mirror in which the figure on the right of frame is reflected. The spaces of foreground and background are very clearly delineated: they are quite literally bordered by the portrait's (un-bordered) paintings. Such a clearly marked division has the effect of flattening both planes, the foreground especially. Under this sort of scrutiny, the notion that one figure in the foreground could be the reflection of another figure in the foreground becomes implausible. Yet our exploded readings linger on (they always do). For us, there is still a mirror in the left of the frame. It is facing the camera. If it is facing the camera, then its reflection must belong to the photographer. If the reflection belongs to the photographer, then its resemblance to the subject of the photograph (still to right of the frame) is uncanny. He must be the photographer himself and this must be a self-portrait. ('Photography is a means of appropriating something,' wrote Sontag.) As our exploded readings start to disintegrate (they always do), our understanding of this portrait as a self-portrait adds a further richness to the picture. The image to the left of the frame, which we imagined and have now un-imagined as a mirror, is cast *en abyme* as it once again assumes its status as a work of art. Is it a study for the photograph in which it appears? Or has this photograph somehow caught itself in the very process of developing? It would not surprise me. This is, after all, a portrait that develops as none of the others do. Why did Cartier-Bresson go to such lengths to make it so?

'The original way in which the work of art was embedded in the context of tradition was through worship,' said Walter Benjamin. Within the Christian tradition, however, the image was initially viewed with suspicion, even horror. Lycomedes, a disciple of John, had a portrait of his master painted in secret so that he could worship it in his cell. 'I see that thou art still living in heathen fashion,' John reprimands him upon discovery. 'This that thou hast now done is childish and imperfect: thou hast drawn a dead likeness of the dead.' It was not until the conversion of Constantine in 312AD, when the coming of Christ was deemed to have concluded the Mosaic prohibition, that images started to appear in monasteries and churches. 'God had finally shown himself in an image,' writes Hans Belting. 'Only this wasn't a made image, but a body. Images, when finally they began to circulate, drew their authority first and foremost from this body. Those that later came to be designated as true were true inasmuch as they attested the true body of Christ.' In the Orthodox tradition, the icon became a devotional object. There, the image itself is worshipped in the belief that it can transmit devotional energies to its subject if made according to certain pictorial conventions. An icon is a window into heaven. Its maker must use a technique known as 'inverse perspective' to depict this heavenly space as infinite. 'The Son of God become man could not be presented as one who had become so confined in the limits of the body that the universe was left empty of His government.'

But left empty is was. God is dead, said Nietzsche, and although an exact time was never given, we know His death corresponds pretty closely to the invention of photography. Within just a few years, it had altered the way people looked at the world. By 1853 Feuerbach was already noting that: 'our era prefers the image to thing, the copy to the original, the representation to the reality, the appearance to being.' Photography is a magical activity, the photograph a cultic object. It has been related to death, to the work of mourning, even to prophecy. Photography stops time. Balzac would not allow his picture to be taken because he feared *it* would take *him*. Hugo made sure his picture was taken. He believed it would make him. Each author's approach offers its own concession to the power of photography, a power arising from its particular relation to truth. Here, for the first time, were images created not by hand, but by machine, by technology. A photograph is a literal emanation of its referent. To look at a photo of Giacometti (who else?) is to be a witness to actual traces passed onto film by the sculptor's own body. The photograph constitutes a 'certificate of presence.' It is true inasmuch as it attests the true body of the referent. The camera was infallible. It replaced the eye of God. People believed in Photography.

At around the same time, artists and writers assumed the role of secular saints, inviting the world to view their work as in some way sacred. In this reading, art was something that could bypass mere daily doings and go straight to the essence of things. Cézanne could plunge into the depths, it was said, 'and fix upon the secret of Being in a few abstract lines.' In Russia, Kazimir Malevich claimed his non-objective art offered access to a so-called 'fourth dimension.' 'The drawing of a cross for the first Christians is for us the drawing of a square,' said his protégé, El Lissitzky. 'This is the new faith.' It was no mere revolutionary dogma. In the United States, Abstract Expressionism made its own appeals to the spirit. 'Instead of making cathedrals out of Christ, man, or 'life,' wrote Barnett Newman, 'we are making them out of ourselves, out of our own feelings." Such exalted claims were by no means limited to the visual arts. Rimbaud saw himself as a seer. Yeats said the work of a writer was 'a blind struggling in the network of stars.' Brecht viewed art as a means of spiritual transformation. This is all old hat at this point. But whatever we might think of these claims (and personally, I don't think very much of them), the fact that they were made remains.

God died and an infrastructure of saints collapsed. Then the pantheon moved in. It was left to the photographers of the age to 'canonise' those writers and artists who, directly or indirectly, sought to occupy the vacancy. Nadar gave it a shot. So did Steichen, Avedon and André Kertész. Their attempts were admirable, in a way. But the work was never allegorical enough for iconography. It posed too many enigmas. Cartier-Bresson was different. He photographed everyone worth photographing in a style that, like the icons of the Russian Orthodox tradition, conformed to a strict geometry in order to portray with complete economy the life and work of his subjects. His catalogue is a 'canon' of the twentieth century. Nobody's work embodied the term quite as fully. But in so 'canonising' these figures, he placed them under his camera's rule. Unlike the Russian Orthodox tradition, where holy figures are portrayed as unconfined, Cartier-Bresson's sitters are nearly always depicted indoors, enclosed, imprisoned. Is it any wonder that cigarettes have such a high symbolic currency in these portraits? Christian Bérard is even placed behind bars.

Nothing is transmitted beyond his concretised frames. There is no 'beyond.' His subjects are imprisoned in their own image, their image fetishised at the expense of the work. The idea of the Author, this figure of 'genius' responsible for the work, is introduced before the work ever gets an airing.

Has anybody read even a single one of Pound's Cantos since Cartier-Bresson took his portrait in 1971? I sincerely doubt it. But if by chance some wet petal on a bough (or was it a *black petal*? a *wet bough*? a *pet bow*? who knows?) contrived to move beyond the image, they would find the work already changed, diminished, singularised. Barthes said that to give a text an author is 'to impose a limit on that text, to furnish it with a final signified, to close the writing.' To give an author an image in the manner of Cartier-Bresson has much the same effect. A limit imposed on the author. They are furnished with a final signified. There is no longer Ezra Pound, only Cartier-Bresson's 'Ezra Pound.' Did Cartier-Bresson know the damage he was doing?

To give a text *an image of an author* is to appropriate the text, to reduce it to a singular set of photographic conventions. It is to smother the text not with a final signified, but with a final signified of a final signified. I look at Giacometti's sculptures, I look at them closely, and all I see is him crossing the road in the rain. It has become an utter tautology to say the image of Giacometti looks like his own work. The image *is* the work. It belongs to the photographer now. His photos even tell us so. Did you notice anything strange, for instance, about that other Giacometti portrait, the one so evocative of touch, of fingertips, of sculpture? The sculptor's own fingers play no part in this sculpted scene. They have been put away, pocketed, concealed. It would not surprise me to learn they had been broken. 'Technologies of inscription and the undoing of certain protocols of reading, writing, and thinking that they occasion must be thought together,' said Gerhard Richter, introducing Derrida. 'In addition to the affirmative, gathering, preserving dimension of the archive, there is *the violence of the archive itself, as archive, as archival violence.*' Diminished in this way, artistic work has ceased to matter. Is it any wonder the portrait catalogues of Cartier-Bresson's successors (Mapplethorpe, Leibovitz, Bailey) are all filled up with celebrities, of images *qua* images? At least Warhol was up front about his workings; at least he placed himself within it.

Cartier-Bresson never sat for his own self-portrait. He let others do that for him. Naturally, he knew the damage he was doing. So did Derrida. He'd understood quite early, in fact. 'What I was writing had to lead both socially and politically to the defetishisation of the author, especially the author as they appear according to the photographic code.' He took steps to protect the work, forbidding all public photographs of himself until, in the late-1970s, a year or two after Cartier-Bresson was said to have 'retired,' the prohibition was finally lifted. Cartier-Bresson never took his photograph, which perhaps explains why his work seems so difficult to a society literate only in the image. He was not the only one to have taken caution, in any case. In 1946, Cartier-Bresson arrived at Paul Valéry's house only to find the poet 'formally dressed as a member of the *Académie francaise* rather than as himself.' In this ridiculous get-up, Valéry stood next to a bust of his own head that he'd positioned on a mantelpiece in front of a mirror. The picture is such a mess that it is often cited as an example of how collaboration with the sitter doesn't work. But Valéry was a figure who 'never stopped calling into question and deriding the Author.' Was he really 'collaborating' with the photographer? Hardly. His portrait is a send-up of the form. Others were a little slower to understand, but it seems clear that word eventually got out in certain circles. 'Today the more the author's figure invades the field,' wrote Italo Calvino in 1959, 'the more the world he portrays empties; then the author himself fades, and one is left with a void on all sides.' Colette, Eisler, Brok and Aragon obscure their faces accordingly. Colette even sits with a companion. But it was all too little, too late. I look at Giacometti's sculptures, I look at them closely, and all I see is him crossing the road in the rain. His coat is pulled over his head. But is he really looking for shelter? Or is he looking for a place to hide? In that decisive moment he came close to disappearing, but he did not come close enough. He was snapped, trapped, a monk in the rain. His hiding became his habit and his habit became his icon and his icon hides the work. It has disappeared completely now. Man keeps walking, but he walks with a void on all sides.

Close to the Edit
The films of Nicolas Roeg by Richard Kovitch

> 'The motion picture is still such a magical and mysterious combination of reality, art, science and the supernatural—as well as the gateway to the nature of Time, and perhaps even the first clue in solving the puzzle of what we're doing here on this world.' – Nicolas Roeg

Born the 15th August 1928, director Nicolas Roeg has been alive almost as long as cinema has mixed sound and vision to such hypnotic effect. His career began amidst the austere gloom of post-war Britain. 'In those days getting a job at a studio was like getting a job in a factory,' he notes in his memoir *The World Is Ever Changing*.[1] This was an era before film schools and theory influenced the medium. Work fixated upon the industrial; the application of machinery and technical knowledge to document stories. But it was from learning this trade, by immersing himself in the industry's conventions, that Roeg would come to challenge the methods of working, and from there 'the art grew.'

Roeg's formative years were spent at De Lane Lea on Wardour Street before he moved to MGM at Borehamwood. He was originally a camera operator, then a focus puller, then cinematographer. He worked with the greats and observed them, always learning, always inquisitive. Roger Corman's *Masque Of Red Death*, David Lean's *Lawrence Of Arabia*, François Truffaut's *Fahrenheit 451*—'it was a magical time, mysterious' and underlined to Roeg how much more there is

---

1 Nicolas Roeg, *The World Is Ever Turning*, Faber & Faber, (2013)

to film than merely writing, theatre and photography. 'Oscars are won with two or three shots,' he told the *Guardian* in 2005.[2] It is emotion that burns on the memory: the human face, the panoramic view, the instant when image and sound combine to create moments of triumph or defeat. Roeg extrapolates on this: 'An image makes more emotional sense than words because it helps the imagination on its way visually rather than just by interpretation.' Films show, they don't tell, even if—in the case of Roeg—what they show is elusive and illusory.

Roeg's directing career began in 1968, when he made *Performance* alongside Donald Cammell. It is fitting that a film about the mutability of identity not only has two directors but that their collaboration was so total their influence is impossible to distinguish in the final cut. The film began with a script by the inexperienced Cammell, who sought Roeg's expertise as co-director and camera operator. Cammell originally conceived *Performance* as a 'light hearted romp.' The final film was anything but. After exchanging ideas with actor/gangster David Litvinoff, the tone of Cammell's script quickly darkened, as London's street level blur between show business and crime found its voice. Roeg's camera added a further layer of imagery that exploded colour and voyeurism in every direction. Much maligned upon its release by critics and the studio who financed it—Warner Bros presumed they were getting *A Hard Day's Night* (1964), albeit with the Rolling Stones—the film's release was delayed for over two

---

[2] Jason Wood, the *Guardian*, Friday 3 June 2005. Nicolas Roeg at Hay Film Festival transcript: http://www.theguardian.com/film/2005/jun/03/hayfilmfestival2005.hayfestival

years as re-edits and law suits flew. Legend has it when the Warner Brothers executives finally saw it one of the wives in attendance 'vomited in shock.' It caused lead actor James Fox to walk out on his film career, propelled into Evangelical Christianity by a toxic mix of his father's death, smoking the hallucinogen DMT and the stress of playing Chas. '*Performance* gave me doubts about my way of life,' he noted ominously. For filmmakers it marked something equally as significant: the moment British film finally mirrored the dramatic social shifts of post-war culture. It was a frenzy of ideas; a kaleidoscopic vision of a culture in flux—a film about vice. And Versa.' So radical was its impact that forty years later critic Mark Cousins would note in his acclaimed fifteen-hour documentary *The Story Of Film* (2012), 'if any movie in the whole *Story of Film* should be compulsory viewing for film makers, maybe this is it.'

Part Artaudian identity crisis, part Borgesian psychosis, *Performance* also established the signature themes that would preoccupy Roeg for the rest of his career and liberate him from the lethargic thinking that had marked his formative years in the industry. Dread, sexuality, the uncanny, alienation and identity—all are explored in provocative fragments, then spliced together into a dream-like whole as coherent as it is elusive. Roeg felt he was emulating Max Ernst in this respect, creating 'utterly strange things from the utterly familiar.' Revisiting his work today, two things strike you. The first is his ability to elicit great performances from rock stars—Mick Jagger, David Bowie and Art Garfunkel. Few directors can claim casting a pop star was a great decision. Roeg can claim a hat trick. Second, that visually Roeg is one of cinema's most distinctive and original practitioners. His films operate as mosaics, elliptical and distorted, a series of crash zooms and crosscutting propelled by emotion and imagery, less linear storytelling and reason. All editors fragment time and space to propel a film's narrative, but most try to disguise it. Roeg does it explicitly to make a philosophical point.

Through the 1970s this approach to film would establish Roeg as one of Britain's greatest film makers. From *Performance* to *Eureka* (1983) he delivered a body of work that continues to mesmerise, even as its mysteries deepen. There is a curious British kink that pulses through Roeg's work. He likes to watch, not least his then real-life wife Theresa Russell, whom he has filmed countless explicit sex scenes with, with many different leading men. This perversity was there from the start; he took Jenny Agutter, star of TV's *The Railway Children* (1968), stripped her of her school uniform and filmed her swimming naked in the lagoons of the Australian outback. He filmed such an intimate sex scene with Julie Christie and Donald Sutherland in *Don't Look Now* (1973) that Christie's then lover Warren Beatty pressurised Warner Bros to cut the scene from the film.[3] Suspicions that Christie and Sutherland had really fucked were encouraged by *Variety* editor Peter Bart, amplifing the rumour and elevating a bleak, occult thriller into a box office success. In *The Man Who Fell To Earth* (1976), Candy Clark (Roeg's then girlfriend) has alienating sex with David Bowie, before urinating on the floor when the Thin White Duke shape shifts before her eyes. In *Bad Timing* (1980)—'a terrifying love story'—Art Garfunkel fucks

---

3 Mark Sanderson, *Don't Look Now*, BFI Classics (2012)

Theresa Russell's recently deceased body in a desperate bid to possess her one last time. The impotent rage of Oliver Reed in *Castaway* (1985), the Oedipal incest at the heart of *Track 29* (1988), the earthy lust that drives *Puffball* (2007): sex and anxiety are regular bedfellows in Roeg's work, entangled but conjoined, as desperate as they are beautiful.

But as Roeg testifies in his memoir—itself shapeless, random, but always compelling—'time' has long been his greatest obsession. Its malleability hypnotises him. His moment of revelation that within the arts only film could truly explore this topic arrived when he was working with editor Anthony Gibbs on Richard Lester's *Petula* (1968), a dark, non-linear drama that saw Julie Christie and George C. Scott falling away from each other in Flower Power-era San Francisco. This non-linearity is the calling card of Roeg's subsequent films, the first of which, *Performance* and *Walkabout*, were cut by Gibbs. In his memoir, Roeg recalls his thrill at discovering the Editola—a primitive, reel-to-reel dubbing machinery—whilst working at De Lane Dea. It enabled him to play footage both forwards and backwards, even displace sound, and revealed how shifts in speed could alter 'reality'. The experience expanded Roeg's thoughts dramatically on what a film might be: 'I realised there was another way of telling stories, of passing on information—not on the page but through the retention of the image, the moving image.' In *Walkabout*—marketed as 'a place where time stands still'— two children (Jenny Agutter and Lucien John) find themselves disorientated by the infinite space that envelops them in the Australian outback after their father has committed suicide. The key image that expresses Roeg's obsession with time is the scene in which the kangaroo is killed. As its body falls, the film reverses and it is seemingly brought back to life. 'We were showing what's going on in the imagination,' explains Roeg. Gibbs went on to edit *Performance* and *Walkabout*. The language of cinema had taken another great step.

Roeg's preoccupation with the editor is worth emphasising in an era where the credit for film still remains unjustly carved up between the director, performer and writer. If you remain unconvinced of the relatively low esteem the editor is held in by the wider public, then consider how many famous editors you can actually name. A movie fan might muster Walter Murch, Thelma Schoonmaker and Dede Allen; the wider public would have drawn a blank long before. And yet the editor is arguably as crucial to shaping the film the audience will encounter as even the director. To understand the editing process is to understand what distinguishes film from all other art forms. It is also key to understanding Roeg's work.

> 'The notion of directing a film is the invention of critics - the whole eloquence of cinema is achieved in the editing room.' – Walter Murch[4]

The history of ideas are difficult to trace, but Roeg's signature, non-sequential editing style—most brilliantly expressed in the sex scene with Donald Sutherland and Julie Christie in *Don't Look Now*— has its origins in productions that Roeg was involved in prior to his directing career, not least the films of Richard Lester, edited by Antony Gibbs. Gibbs

---

4 Walter Murch, *In The Blink Of An Eye: A Perspective on Film Editing* (2001)

delivered the original edit of *Performance* in 1968; the version finally released was re-cut in L.A. over the following two years by Donald Cammell with editor Frank Mazzola, who was responsible for the film's highly revered opening sequence. What this serves to illustrate is how collaborative the making of a film is and how quickly radical new ideas can take hold and spread. Indeed, late 60s Hollywood sees a proliferation of this rapid cut style in several key films —Dede Allen's work in *Bonnie & Clyde* (1967), Lou Lomabardo's work in *The Wild Bunch* (1969), Donn Cambern's work in *Easy Rider* (1969)—as the radical style of Godard and *La Nouvelle Vague* finally infiltrated the cutting rooms of Hollywood, though as Dede Allen illuminates, all these techniques had originally been pioneered in the 1920s by Russian filmmakers such as Sergei Eisenstein, Dziga Vertov and Vsevolod Pudovkin.

Roeg's celebration of the editor as a lynchpin of the cinematic process not only sends praise to a much under sung profession, but it also helps us to understand what a film really is. Stanley Kubrick cited editing as being the only craft exclusive to filmmaking: 'I love editing. I think I like it more than any other phase of filmmaking. If I wanted to be frivolous, I might say that everything that precedes editing is merely a way of producing film to edit.' For anyone who has ever inhabited an edit suite for a prolonged period of time, Kubrick's assertions will strike a chord. It is a womb-like environment, isolated from the chaos of everyday life, where craft and technology can transform incoherent, disconnected images and sounds into a dream-like whole, capable of conveying both intense emotion and meaning. How the editor interacts with the material is open to differing practice.⁵ Some editors disregard the script after a preliminary read and try and make sense of the story from the rushes alone. Others have been on set and taken notes. Most begin editing the film long before the director has finished shooting, shaping it in solitude far removed from the wider mayhem of the production. This is why coverage —the amount of footage there is to work with in the edit —is a key obsession of directors and editors alike.⁶ Without coverage, they limit the options in the edit. Roeg reiterates this point, 'Shoot a lot. Never say 'cut'. In the edit you can live the film again.'

> 'Scripts are very curious things. I mean, they very rarely—I can't stress this enough—reflect what is the final movie. You can't see the beauty on the page.' – Nicolas Roeg

If the editor of the film ultimately controls the story, where does that leave the writer? There are still major misunderstandings about what a screenplay is, which is why so many problems arise in assessing its importance to the final film. As Colin MacCabe notes,[7] a screenplay's definition remains 'bizarre and elusive,' and there is still no agreed format it should take. Significantly, the function of a screenplay mutates depending

---

[5] *The Cutting Edge: The Magic of Movie Editing* (2004) (98 min), dir. Wendy Apple

[6] Film Editing: Jarrod Walker takes us round the mind of a film editor: http://www.closeupfilm.com/features/filmmaking/filmediting.htm

[7] Donald Cammell, edited by Colin MacCabe, *Performance*, Faber & Faber (2001)

upon who is reading it. For the financiers at the studio, it is an outline of what the film can potentially be and whether it can be marketed (this is why studios now prefer two-page treatments followed by a forty-five to sixty word 'scriptment' as it minimises read time). For the actors it gives them lines to say and intimates emotions to convey (although dialogue and actions will ultimately be finalised in performance). For the director it's a list of scenes to film (though as Roeg notes there are so many variables during production much of what is shot will be spontaneous). This is why Roeg refuses to storyboard, because he does not want to circumnavigate chance. Mistakes are honoured as hidden intentions. Indeed, it is worth remembering that many of cinema's greatest moments—'You talkin' to me,' 'We're going to need a bigger boat,' Indiana Jones shooting the swordsmen, 'I'll have what she's having' etc—weren't scripted and materialised through performance. For this reason Roeg warns against making the screenplay too complete in case 'there's no room for anyone else.'

There are also the enduring myths that a bad screenplay will automatically make a bad film. Harrison Ford may have lamented of the *Star Wars* screenplay 'you can type this shit, but you sure can't say it' but the film's visuals enabled it to transcend any literary shortcomings that were on the page. That a great screenplay will make a great film is another perception, yet Cormac McCarthy's revered screenplay for *The Counsellor* (2013) has somehow resulted in 'the worst film ever made,' according to several critics. And we are still led to believe by the screenwriting industry that a screenplay provides the film's structure. Yet Quentin Tarantino's full script for *Django Unchained* (2013) ran to a rambling five and a half hours coverage, where as the final film—still arguably thirty minutes too long—had been edited down to just two and a half hours. Screenplays change explains Roeg because 'life changes, locations change, everything changes—dictated by the money and the finance.'

Still, Roeg has worked with many great writers and cherishes their contributions to his work. No wonder. It is an extraordinary list that includes Edward Bond, Daphne Du Maurier, Paul Mayersberg, Dennis Potter, Roald Dahl, Joseph Conrad, Edgar Allen Poe and Fay Weldon. Bond believes his screenplay for *Walkabout* remains 'the best thing I've done.' That it amounted to fourteen pages of notes—just vivid descriptions of scenes—adds further irony. Inevitably, Twentieth Century Fox were unimpressed with this and demanded embellishment. To secure financing Roeg reluctantly expanded the notes to about fifty pages. The truth is the film really began when the cameras started to roll in the Australian outback. 'We found the film as we made it,' Roeg later reflected. This is really how a film materialises. When movies are successful the director transcends the writer's presence (*Walkabout, Don't Look Now*), when they're less successful the writer's hand stays present (Dennis Potter's screenplay for *Track 29*). Film ultimately remains a director's medium, irrespective of the extent to which the director must collaborate to achieve their vision. If there is no governing vision, the film will fail to impose itself. As writer Ian McEwan once lamented, fed up with the lack of influence a writer could exert on a film production, a screenplay is 'at best a recipe. The cooking really begins with the filming and editing.'

With all this mutability in mind, it is no wonder screenwriters often feel marginalised from the process. They know that whoever edits the film ultimately controls the film. The writer is at the wrong end of the production line. Similarly, actors know that an editor can build a performance. Early test screenings for *Basic Instinct* (1992) rejected Sharon Stone's delivery as hammy; after re-cuts test audiences declared her a star. An actor may assume 'take 5' was their best take and the one selected for inclusion. The editor will know the final scene was actually amalgamated from every take, trimming the best bits from the coverage and stitching them together anew. When to cut is as vital as when not to cut. Individual frames take on the importance of musical notes. Editing is a process of composition. The final film should flow like a symphony, not divide into chapters like a novel. This has always been Roeg's approach and he cannot state the point enough. 'Film has nothing to do with theatre because the theatre is driven by language—but film is not driven by language, it's driven by image. Images drive the plot, images drive the action. Words cover up a lot of embarrassment, truths, inner thoughts, all kinds of things - but cinema works in a completely different way. Our stories move forwards on a lateral not a linear fashion.'

> 'No one sums up the decline of British cinema better than Nicolas Roeg—from *Performance* to Guy Ritchie.'
> – Mark Fisher.[8]

8 'You Remind Me of Gold: Dialogue with Simon Reynolds,' (Originally published in *Kaleidoscope* magazine, 2010): http://markfisherreblog.tumblr.com/post/32185314385/you-remind-me-of-gold-dialogue-with-simon-reynolds

In his later years, Roeg's career lost its momentum; it is no coincidence that this was after *Heaven's Gate* (1980) nearly bankrupted United Artists, ushering in a period when the studios re-instated their tight control on the process. Accountants and focus groups accrued greater power. The marketing spend increased. The movie poster became as important as the film it was promoting. Roeg continued to work but his obsessions were checked, even if the themes were retained. The explicit eroticism of *Hotel Paradise* (1995) (which contains the line, 'You did not fuck a swan—but you sure came close'), the unearthly drift of *The Sound Of Claudia Schiffer* (2005), the unsettling experimentalism of *Puffball*, much maligned by critics yet packing images so powerful they are impossible to erase (not least the explosion of sperm into Kelly Reilley's womb at the climax of an explicit sex scene). This desire to dwell on the essence of things suggests Roeg was a frontrunner of filmmakers such as David Lynch, David Cronenberg and Gaspar Noe, men fixated with the very pulse of existence, even as his early lead was pegged back by more restrained, later work (*Castaway*, *The Witches* (1990), *Cold Heaven* (1991)).

Yet Roeg's influence still serves as a gateway to understanding the present. In the internet age, we increasingly perceive culture to be non-linear. As the critic Simon Reynolds has observed, this is 'a world of flattened out temporality.' Everything is present all of the time. New art is presented alongside old art. We look backwards and forwards simultaneously. For modernists this shift in perception presents a challenge; the visible state of progress they demand of culture—of rejecting the old in the quest for the new—

has collapsed in on itself. Everything is consumed laterally. Any sense of teleology has been obfuscated. Everyone is an editor now. The experience of communication on-line is not dissimilar to the cross-cutting that defines Roeg's best films; they pre-empt this way of seeing, preparing us for the here and now by presenting information all at once, rather than unfolding it sequentially. These flash frames and bursts of data evoke the way information is presented on-line—one hundred and forty characters or less, six second Vines, endless Tumblrs that stockpile image after image after image without chronology or clear links—yet these are all traits that dominate the unfolding chaos of Roeg's greatest work.

No wonder then, among contemporary filmmakers, his work continues to resonate and inspire. He remains a pioneer who imposed upon cinema a distinct, new way of seeing. As Roeg once explained to a Studio Executive who feared the audience would be confused, 'They won't get it, Nic.' 'No, they'll get it; it's you who's not getting it, because you're trying to force something that's different into being the same.' Being the same is not something Nicolas Roeg could ever be accused of and therein lies his greatness. He is a different type of film maker, but one who makes more sense now than at any time in his long career.

Oslo, Norway
An extract from a novel by John Holten

Let us not ask then for now or for something for nothing, what was is consigned to the world and what wasn't is consigned to time. To be, is easy. Not to be, is difficult. Let us move toward being then. The end is something none of us know intimately in the present. But it's straight up ahead, look no further than the bottom of this page.

Nothingness.

The ends.

Until such time that they all begin again.

The destruction of worlds, all that extinction and more, the slowing currents of our sun. The Higgs boson, the extraction of oil, gold. Let us embrace nothingness and try to fill it with being because in our ever-increasing specialised imaginations we trundle toward nothing and absence not with any ceremony or sanctity but blindly. Our domain over matter, things, people, is only ever a progression toward our own doom, inevitably bringing us down, away from the light of our roiling sun, into the empty space of a world unfurling. Walking up an escalator in the wrong direction, against the current in a shopping centre.

Let us introduce a street. It is dark with figures moving down its incline. It is in the east of a city, connecting neighbourhoods. The figures are returning home, their hands touch each other, entwine. A smile in the dark.

We are and we will not be, the line between is what makes up our life.

What the rain doesn't say but shows.

A year of solo love.

To be and not to be, on this street.

•

In the old Nordic stories of Ragnarök that weave together to tell about the twilight of the gods, the end of the world, Loki at a certain moment goes into a place known as the Iron Wood and meets a giant who is composed of anguish, Angurboda, and rapes her. Then in her mercurial dolour, she gives birth to a wolf-cub, a snake and a giantess. Odin, Loki's old friend, sent a force to deal with these dangerous creatures, setting in course the events that would lead to the death of the gods, to the flattening of the world in darktime and fire. The snake was banished into the sky before falling back down into the depths of the ocean; the giantess was reduced to a fog of the dead, a hell.

The wolf, Fenris, was not to be killed for that wasn't how the story was premeditated: Odin could only neutralise Fenris until such time the gods set about their own destruction. Until the time of the wolf was upon them all. Fenris was bound in three different chains, the first two he broke with his strength before he was bound by a fetter that dwarves had welded.

Camilla dated Trifke for around six months. She called him Tronno, her 'silly little Tronno,' because the name sounded unbearably foreign to her, and one night they slept together with Sybille, the latter recognising neither herself, her friend nor least of all the Serb during their time in bed together. Only this did not happen: the event passed into meaninglessness at the same time it happened, it was part of her life but also it was not. They had returned home after a night downtown and the three of them had been in Camilla's apartment, all drunk and the Serb and Camilla had worked themselves hard on cocaine, when the two girls started to make out. When all three were in bed the sex was perfunctory, dull. An act of the past that became in their story, the story of William and Sybille, like the wolf-cub Fenris, tethered and taunted, waiting to unleash the end of things that had to end.

One evening in March they were having dinner in Hell's Kitchen and Camilla rang on the phone, crying. William stopped eating his pizza and looked at Sybille, and could see what he thought was a darkness descend over her eyes, nose, down to the shallow of her throat. But then it was gone and he had to ask what was wrong, he couldn't calculate or interpret an imagined darkness, a brief shadow of fear.

Oh just this fucking ex-boyfriend she has. He's giving her trouble.

Why?

Because he's in trouble.

There weren't many clues, but they would become enough. He added them together over the course of some weeks. Simple questions gave bottom-heavy answers: Camilla's fickle interest in the absurd and extreme led her to a drug dealer; Sybille's will to impress Camilla led her into bed with them. In the months that followed William was left with thought and memory, two black ravens following him around the dusk-stained streets of Oslo, asking then for now in bitter scraws of miscalculated nostalgia.

The street was dark and they were walking down it toward Grønland. A Muslim man walked by after evening prayer and crossed the street in a small jog, passed into shadow and was gone. Further down somebody shouted in Urdu an entreaty but they were nowhere to be seen.

Lights from the buildings seeped yellow into the orange of the streetlights. Sybille smiled. William was lost in thought, his face flat. Memories that weren't his own didn't cease in being calculated into convictions. Their fingers touched, searched for a hook. Ahead a figure approached them whose silhouetted outline was menace itself.

Sybille stopped smiling. This was a meeting of paths that shouldn't happen, despite the feeling that it was somehow pre-ordained. William recognised the Serb straightaway, as if his thoughts blended perfectly with memories that weren't his own, a photo on Facebook, Camilla laughing in some west Oslo bar, her arms around a middle-aged man who smirked at the camera, knowing well that he shouldn't be where he was but didn't care about the impropriety. All three slowed their steps and in the dark of gloaming the same smirk appeared. Their hands released themselves. William's fury was bred by sadness, an inarticulate sadness made from thought and memories, the cheeky pursuit of two hopping ravens.

Hello Sybille, the Serb said, almost laughing. They stood facing each other. William's hand moved ahead of his mind, on it's own and slapped him across the face.

A slap that would bring about the fall, an end.

It's always there with you, your past. Weighing heavy on thoughts and actions—invisible—dark and in shadow. It doesn't need to be always like this, but sometimes it refuses to be otherwise. I sit thinking of these two people, and of her of course, trying to configure a version of the past that sits easily in the present.

Perhaps it is a wrong turn brought about by the sandstone of Spain, of being too far south in Iberia, but it is difficult not to think of Alan Pauls' novel *The Past*. Not that Pauls is from Spain: he's from Argentina, and *The Past* is a novel of Buenos Aires, a place I've never been although Sybille has and perhaps you have too? What's important is that *The Past* could happen anywhere, possibly, with the exception of those places that are rooted in the daily art of survival, that is to say a large part of the world. Memory, thought—these are superfluous luxuries, and when they are separated from society and dealt with by individuals alone it is so often hard to see them as nothing more than masochistic luxuries. In the novel by Pauls the sex comes to you as arid, sore, dry-humping. You don't have the book to consult: the female protagonist's obsession could be a blueprint for William's (however her's is incessant (though offscreen somewhat, manic, slightly threatening)) while the nihilism of the male protagonist—what was his name? Ralph? Romeo? Something French you think[1]—echoes that of Sybille, but then again not really, for her efforts in nihilism are for Camille's benefit only. They're unsure of themselves, but then what do unsure nihilistic efforts look like exactly, in real life? I must remember to be careful with what I say to you and how I say it.

Anyway it's one of the few books you had to put aside for the sheer physical upset and nausea it stirred in you: reading it was like looking on at a car crash of a relationship, in slow motion, unfolded over the course of years that were badly

---

[1] Some months later you consult the book: his name is Rimini.

out of focus (that ruined monument: the past!), dense pages passing through the stupidity—dogged and insistent—of a life lived with all the normal twists and turns and decisions of fools in love. You read it weeping.

But what are you weeping over? The novel is about a couple who have been together since their teenage years and who in their late twenties decide to break up. He is a translator, and she is some kind of social worker, under the influence of a despotic lesbian guru figure who seems to hate men, men just like the translator. So they break up, divide up their life together. He gets on with things, lives his life, translates, has new relationships, does loads of cocaine (there are perhaps the best fifty pages you have ever read about drugs in this book, reading it one feels like the character, the writer, the translator (from the original Spanish) and in turn you, the reader, are all on cocaine without realising it). The book becomes somewhat exhilarating and terrifying. You mean to say the book becomes physical, reading it is visceral, enervating. The ex-girlfriend finds the translator's ability to get on with his affairs abominable and it seems to eat her from the inside, adding up to the cliché of fury having no hell like a spurned woman. She acts somewhat psychotic. Almost dies. Falls to pieces. Comes back together again while ultimately it is the translator who is falling to pieces. She remains friends with his father like a lifeline, constantly off stage but you know she's not far away, flapping around and about to cause a scene (at one point she causes a car crash while following the translator after a public conference). But he too falls apart one too many times. Succumbs to the unnamed power of the past. And then in the end they get back together. The point maybe being: the past is too strong to let go, it'll catch up with us all eventually. They go off into the city together, happy ever after. You think. Perhaps this is all being misremembered, being given the wrong reading. Books too after all, and the stories they contain, belong to the past, to what was then, made up and read about in the gone before. The lies of fools in love.

Geographist, that was the word used. It came through to me the other day by way of a text message to my phone and I stared at it for some time trying to figure out how I felt about this word. It came from a woman who I had spent time with in bars the week before. All my days I'm surrounded by an English that is bold, worldly and intermittently (though in fact rather consistently if I think about it) entirely incorrect. This language of an adopted English is the language in which I fall in love: nobody I have loved spoke the same language as I and the consequences can be seen in this story.

Geographist. I'm in Spain. Drunkenly walking through Valencia's Carmen district with Lorenzo 'El Mapas' Sandoval and I'd like to draw attention to this nickname: The Map. We walk down the narrow streets and around corners and the buildings rise up above us, they clutch to the little alleyways and seem almost to slope outward as if their roofs were trying to embrace, much like rue au Maire in Paris, an important street in my biography. But before we go further into this dark maze I must insist that you don't get the wrong idea, I love this language, the lingua franca of the age, because it makes me work: I have to situate myself in the world and relate to many languages through one—Norwegian, German,

French, Spanish, Italian—thanks to their influence on the bastard child English.

'Hey El Mapas, where did you get the name El Mapas from?'

'Paco, my friend, he gave it to me the other night. You were there, don't you remember you drunken fool, in that bar in Benimaclet.'

'I don't remember,' I said, ignoring the barb, 'but why did he give it to you?',

'I don't know. Are you jealous?' And he laughed with that laugh of his, El Mapas, his whole body joining in for the fun of it. 'You might have the coat Mr Geographist, but you're no map!'

This was preposterous and, I felt, highly unfair on his part, but perhaps it wasn't all that untrue I feared, writing a failed atlas as I was.

'Go fuck yourself El Mapas,' I muttered but all he did was laugh and continue getting me lost in that infernal Moorish labyrinth.

'What are you a map of anyway? You can't just go around calling yourself a map.'

'Why not?'

'Because.'

'I'm a map of every place I've ever loved and I walk with my arms open wide to greet my next love, like this,' and he walked down the alleyway ahead of me with his arms spread wide, 'just like a map… for I am El Mapas! Haven't you read Borges?'

The conversation had become absurd and not, I suspected with a little hesitation, a little dangerous: my Spanish friend and doppelgänger (yes we often get mistaken) had a way of dealing with the world that often threatened to overrule the laws of normality I had tried to instil in myself, the construction I had created in order to deal with the greater unknown, that is the world and everyone in it. Had I read Borges! Pah, I almost let slip about my awful plot in which not only would I read—and reread—Borges, I would rewrite a version of one of his tiny little fictions in such a grandiose way that I would explode the Argentinian's universe (to start with I need only to recall that it's been pointed out with accuracy that Borges spent an entire lifetime travelling the world acting as if people only live and talk for the sake of literature alone, yet sadly we all know that this is far from the case). But I held my breath because these thoughts had raced ahead of me and I had no idea what I was thinking if I'm to be honest, so I knew not how to articulate them: in short I had become scared of my own thoughts.

El Mapas continued to waddle ahead down the middle of whatever abominable *calle* we were on, arms outstretched and his legs trying to walk in a straight line, impossible with the state he was in, and I again muttered to myself, 'Go fuck yourself' until presently we strolled into Plaza del Tossal and El Mapas disappeared into the door of a bar off a side street, where I heard and then saw him being greeted warmly by a man and a woman. I entered meekly behind him.

'Holten!' El Mapas proclaimed to the entire bar, 'come here Holten you fucker. This is John Holten. A geographist from Paris! Look at his green jacket! An explorer of many cities!'

Everyone laughed, including me, hesitantly: the barman and the bar flies, in short the whole bar looked at me and laughed. We were all laughing and drinking beer. And ate countless *pinhxos*, the menacing sounding finger food—not to be confused with tapas—and I thought to myself of all these cities in darkness waiting for a waddling figure, windmill arms outstretched with his timid doppelgänger following up behind him, free men and total fools both: Oslo, Berlin, Paris, Valencia, Dublin, New York, Baltimore, escaping the clutch of literature and the make-belief and searching to embrace the real, the personal, the recognisable territory we stand on with our unsure two feet.

Loki was the third in rankings of the important guys, a troublemaker and shapeshifter, his home was made when empty space was filling with our world. Loki is one of those characters from the northern world and is first encountered when reading about the old stories of nothingness, of ends. The world formed from nothing: first there was space total, a void. Then there were more things, grass, oceans: sooner or later there was Loki.

But we do not know Loki. We know bits of him, and these bits together work toward forming his character in the segues between other stories of gods and beasts.

The gods and their horrendous retinue have returned. And now they call to mind nothing less than our own world, bare and bald and we step into it, with our thoughts and expectations. Sooner or later some get around to calling it god. Some call it a career. Others still a relationship.

Wormhole Sculptor
An interview with Jesse Jones by David Gavan

Jesse Jones treats cultural debris and unrealised histories as if they were the unconscious of our civilisation. Often working through the medium of film, she uses re-enactment as an artistic strategy—a strategy which is filtered through a lens of Brechtian alienation techniques. As with Brecht, the effect she seeks is defamiliarisation. Film, pop culture and politics are conceived of as vessels of shared memory, like a conceptual art version of Carl Jung's collective unconscious.

In *The Struggle Against Ourselves* (2011), Jones collaborates with the CalArts Schools of Film/Video and Theater. The piece traces the oblique genealogy linking the constructivist spectacle of Russian theatre director, Vsevolod Meyerhold (whose artistic vision was influenced by Taylorism and time-and-motion studies), with the capitalist spectacle of Busby Berkeley's scenes of dancing women. Jones also refracts *The Struggle* through the ideas expounded in Siegfried Kracauer's essay, *The Mass Ornament*. This was the title work of a collection of essays, which were published initially in the daily newspaper, *Die Frankfurter Zeitung*, in the Weimar Germany of the twenties and early thirties. The essay brutally exposes the "American distraction factories" that created the Tiller Girls and led on to Berkeley's lavish Hollywood films. *The Struggle Against Ourselves* strikingly super-imposes the Russian avant-garde over high Hollywood with a view to highlighting hidden meanings. The coruscating insight that Jones ends up projecting is that Berkeley's films may be read as an unconscious 'monument' to First World War trauma. Jones reminds us persuasively that Berkeley held the position of artillery lieutenant during that war, and was well-drilled in the art of synchronising group movements.

The artist goes on to make the feasible suggestion that Western popular culture of the 1920s had the (unrealised) chance to become—under Meyerhold's artistic influence—a self-realising inspiration for citizens. In an alternative world, Meyerhold's work could have enlightened the populace in a way similar to the social-conscience-activating plays Bertolt Brecht wrote and staged later in the century. Jones has long been interested in 'how this period of the early 1920s had this amazing potential for a kind of mass culture based on that early socialist cultural optimism.' Instead of a positive relationship between the individual and society, what came into being was the 'lock down' spectacle that Guy Debord describes in *Society of the Spectacle* (1967).

Jones says that she works by instinct (although she has a remarkably keen, and unconventional, intellect), and the strength of her cultural antennae is highly impressive. It can be argued that some artists of Jones's generation (she was born in 1978) might benefit from more outings beyond today's postmodern theme park; that their work would gain depth if they spent as much time immersed in, say, Christopher Marlowe as the multiplex. Certainly, attitudes of cultural relativism (there's a plurality of artistic 'narratives,' and they deserve equal status), and postmodern irony ('this is so bad, it's good') have led to warehouse loads of meretricious and disposable art. However, what pleases about this artist's work is her natural resistance to the facile.

In *The Spectre And The Sphere* (2008), Lydia Kavina—the great niece of Leon Theremin—plays The Internationale on the musical instrument invented by her forebear. Lenin was captivated by Theremin's invention, and, feeling that electronic music would end conservatory elitism, wanted to learn the socialist anthem on it. Theremin left Russia to try and get the instrument into mass production in America, and was later kidnapped by the KGB, and returned to Russia in order to build the first spy technology of the Cold War. History records that Lenin never got his chance at the instrument. In *The Spectre And The Sphere*, Jones presents an alternative history; one in which The Internationale is played on the theremin by a direct descendant of Leon Theremin. Given that this piece of music had been the Stalinist anthem while Kavina's great uncle was under house arrest, Jones' work sought to recuperate the tune.

The camera—which evokes the alien gaze of David Cronenberg's film photography—then glides through the corridors of the Belgian socialist castle, Vooruit (meaning, 'forward'). Constructed in the early twentieth century as a secular, competitive echo of the city's foremost cathedral, the building has been recast as an art centre in recent years. Jones has her conceptual eye on recuperation, and her fixing upon the regeneration of this once-derelict building reflects this recurrent theme in her work.

Presently, a 'Whisper Choir' begins to feverishly recite the communist manifesto. When the alien camera has piloted through to the Vooruit theatre, the sibilant recitation reaches its climax as the camera switches from otherworldly glide to jerk-focus montage. The camera blacks out. In this way, Jones suggests that our neglected cultural and political byways are haunted thoroughfares containing once-possible alternative realities. These spectral avenues may be glimpsed like monuments to potential histories, and Jones's work provides us with the appropriate spectacles.

Other works are driven by an interest in grass roots collaboration that was influenced by Jones's background in political activism. *Zarathustra* (2008) involved a collaboration with the Artane Boy's Band, and entailed their playing the theme from Stanley Kubrick's film, *2001: A Space Odyssey*. This was undertaken in a drained swimming pool in the ruins of Ballymun housing estate. Here, Jones projects the spectre of hope and social regeneration onto the abandoned housing project, with the empty swimming pool acting as a launching pad for future possibilities.

Another compelling collaboration, *12 Angry Films* (2006), saw Jones conducting a series of intensive film and video workshops with a collection of immigrants, along with an assortment of self-enlisted Dublin natives. The project's main feature was the opening of a temporary drive-in cinema in Dublin's Docklands that showed films examining migration, class and social justice. In highlighting the plight of conveniently-ignored individuals, Jones subverts the 'distraction factory' aspects of mass entertainment, as well as the idea of modern art galleries as intellectual adventure playgrounds for the middle classes.

Jesse Jones's current project is *The Prosperity Project*. The work debates the notions of prosperity that sprouted during Ireland's boom years. It does so by engaging with an 'elective' selection of Dublin residents, artists and thinkers.

•

DG In *The Mass Ornament* Siegfried Kracauer writes: 'In order to investigate today's society, one must listen to the confessions of the products of its film industries. They are all blabbing a rude secret, without really wanting to. In an endless sequence of films, a limited number of themes recur again and again: they reveal how society wants to see itself. The quintessence of these films is at the same time the sum of the society's ideologies, whose spell is broken by the interpretation of the themes.'

Your work seems to apply Kracauer's method of analysis, in the way you seem concerned to virtually psychoanalyse popular culture. Why do you feel compelled to sieve through popular culture for the meanings it yields inadvertently?

JJ It's really popular culture that forcibly demands that kind of analysis. As Kracauer says, the story of the Tiller girls almost demands a reply in and of themselves; the 'Shop Girls' demand a reply in and of themselves. But I'm not directed towards analysis through theory, it's more a case of the sensorium of visual culture itself clamouring for a kind of critical attention. In a way there is an intelligence there that I am trying to tap into. I'm trying to find hidden meanings behind these cultural representations; meanings that may cause us to question some other type of wisdom about our society.

I think there's a lot of uncanniness within popular culture, and when you find something just a little bit off —something that registers just a little bit strangely with you—then you can't help but apply a psychoanalytical approach to the subconscious aspects that are at play. So you begin to questions things, from the sensation evoked by the culture itself, you know?

Did you study psychoanalysis at any point? **DG**

No, I studied sculpture, so I view the world in terms of materials. I guess I'm thinking about our culture as a malleable material. But I don't think my artistic role is to create a perspective, or a critique of something that already exists. I physically manipulate pop cultural phenomena, as a material, to see what insights this generates. **JJ**

As if it's a plastic art material—something akin to Play Doh? **DG**

Yeah. *The Struggle Against Ourselves* (2011) doesn't fit that Busby Berkeley and Meyerhold conceit entirely. Or, while it fits in terms of the critical theory, once you start tracing back the relationship between capital and [the Debordian] spectacle, it fits. But, aesthetically and culturally, it's a jam: you're slamming two things together that don't really fit, but it exposes something by creating this 'exquisite corpse' between the historical moments of cultural production. So my background in sculpture influences me in how I can see the materiality of pop culture detritus. I'm asking: 'How can you fuse them together to create a new perspective? A view that questions the cognitive order?' **JJ**

So, you're offering accidental epiphanies? **DG**

JJ I'd say 'instinctive' rather than 'accidental.' It feels instinctive for me to think about Busby Berkeley in relation to Siegfried Kracauer and Vsevolod Meyerhold.

DG Perhaps in keeping with the idea of a postmodern 'global village,' your work has a very international feel. You have said that you would prefer to be considered as an artist, rather than an Irish artist. But you must have been affected by the singular aspects of Ireland. That it's a country that was not colonised by the Romans—despite having their religion—that has not had an industrial revolution—except in the north of Ireland—but does have a capital whose denizens sometimes seem determined to forget Ireland's agricultural background, has been colonised by both England and Roman Catholicism and—perhaps most importantly—is gorging itself at the postmodern pick 'n' mix sweetie stall, without first having digested modernity. That said, it is strange that Ireland is seen by some as a parochial backwater, when you think the premier modernist is James Joyce and the premier proto-postmodernist is Flann O'Brien.

JJ Joyce wrote outside of Ireland as well, so that's partly the answer to your question. Did Joyce privilege being in Ireland and his citizenship within Ireland, or did he privilege being a writer, first and foremost? I think he privileged being a writer, even though so much of his writing was an examination of the relationship between self and nationality. Joyce is really interesting because he addresses the idea of identity, and I think that defining people in terms of nationality is a really reductive response to being in this world. Artistically,

I find the idea of nationality too cumbersome, awkward and inelegant. It doesn't sit well with the expansive or experimental approach to being in the world that writers and artists endeavour to have. So, when I say that my being considered as an Irish artist is not my first priority, that's not to negate my being Irish for any political reasons—it's just that being an artist is so much more important to me. I guess that I'm reminded that I'm Irish because I make so many works outside of Ireland, which inevitably brings me into contact with other cultures.

DG James Joyce's Stephen Dedalus said, 'History is a nightmare from which I am trying to awake.' How far would you agree that many people are so divorced from history nowadays, and beguiled by 'the spectacle'—as well as being seduced by Baudrillard's 'ecstasy of communication'—that it's the aforementioned spectacle that we need to awake from in today's hyperreal, theme park world?

JJ In terms of my work, I'm interested in the stuff that got left behind by the spectacle. I'm interested in re-animating moments that would have fallen by the wayside in lieu of a wider, spectacle-orientated version of culture for mass consumption. In focusing on aspects of meta culture, I look at those things that slide off the mass narrative. The media representation of the Troubles in the 1970s is a case in point. I found myself looking at the Bill McGaw film, *The Steel Shutter* [which documented a 'conflict resolution' group psychotherapy session led by the American psychologist, Carl Rogers, for Northern Irish Catholics and Protestants, in 1973], in relation to that kind of defamiliarisation, as a way of viewing the sectarian divide. That film wasn't focusing on a constructed political narrative in real time; it wasn't mediated by the establishment's version of history. There is such a tension between the construction of historical narrative, and the construction of visual culture, and obviously that's a very political thing. How visual culture is created is clearly a way of creating the proto-historical narrative. The mass media dissemination of a reactionary political narrative—a meta mass culture—has become fragmented in the internet age. Things are more disparate, now.

DG I suppose it's not just the internet that's driving the fragmentation—although it's true that we no longer live in a world where everyone is talking about how funny *The Two Ronnies* was the night before on the bus to work. That disparate thing probably stems from the postmodern atomisation of 'grand narratives' too.

JJ Yes. Postmodernism just exploded that uniform view of history and politics. I'm interested in the detritus, the fall-out from the breaking up of the cultural distractions; in how those distractions institute blind spots when they are set up. I think that what is actually contained in these historical blind spots can be what's real, or more truthful about history.

DG I think that's true. This may be why re-enactment has cropped up so much in the visual arts in recent years. Those who rule get to disseminate their version of history. It ties in with that Michael S. Bennett line[1]: 'Whoever wins the war, gets to write

---

1 In *An Audience with King Richard III*

the history.' So do you mean that, when you watch an inelegantly constructed, ideologically transparent propaganda film, this offers you a chance to psychoanalyse a culture, because you can see how the powerful members of that society wish to be seen?

Yeah, and we are missing something important if we don't value the insights that these cultural documents offer us. Maybe the fact that we don't often value such artefacts tells us something about ourselves. Like that idea of Walter Benjamin's: 'If you want to understand a culture, look at what it leaves out in the garbage, rather than what it places on its plinths.' What do we need? What do we ignore? And what do we devalue and why? These questions are worth asking. **JJ**

It seems to be the case that the internet disseminates the postmodern version of reality, helps spread the hyperreality. How do you feel about the idea that, even as our spectatorship purportedly becomes less passive (we Tweet to live T.V. shows and are incorporated into their content or become famous on YouTube), it controls us more, and does this under the guise of democratisation? **DG**

I think it becomes more dispersed, right? I think the noticeable Facebook factor is how the mass movement of the Tiller Girls has become completely embodied in ourselves. For me, there was definitely a feeling that the dispersal of the spectacle that I was encountering in the modern media was connected to what Kracauer said about the Tiller Girls in the 1920s. What happened with the **JJ**

Tiller Girls was a dispersal of unified synchronicity of the body, where a series of bodies become a unified system of movement, and in a way that could be the internet. We are networked together into a system of synchronised movement and the dissemination of that mass experience is what the spectacle is now. I don't know whether there's anything left to look at, or anything left to be the spectacle. I mean, *X-Factor* is boring: I know people watch it, but they watch it to be part of a group after they have watched it. They watch it so they can talk about it with people the next day. I feel it's shifted from that Cartesian spectacle to a spectacle of [shared] experience.

DG Perhaps this explains the popularity of programmes like *The Apprentice*, and also the rise of site-specific theatre in recent years. There are also those spurious announcements on current affairs programmes about how interested they are to read the viewers' tweets.

JJ Yeah, and I think the internet is what's allowed the Spectacle of shared experience to become pervasive. As much as the mechanised spectacle of mass thought in the twenties allowed for that totalitarian brutality, that relinquishing of responsibility towards a synchronised social body. So there's something about the Tiller Girls, and their synchronised movement, that actually is the internet. But I haven't totally figured that out yet: maybe I need to make an art work about it. That's what I do when I don't understand something. I would either get it completely wrong, or navigate the material in a new way.

You persuasively pointed out the surprising link between **DG** Meyerholdian constructivist spectacle and the capitalist spectacle of [former drill sergeant] Busby Berkeley's films, with their Tiller Girls-evoking dancers. You have also explained how Kracauer's understanding of how the synchronised movements of the Tiller Girls might promote mass conformity gave you the idea to fuse these disparate cultural moments together. How do you feel about the idea that the industrial sound of psytrance music, and the pharmacologically 'wired' bodies pumping away to it in repurposed warehouses (using 'in-group'-endorsed cyber-hippie gestures) show how the intense industrialisation of human labour is echoed in the workers' leisure pursuits?

It's interesting to think of the human desire for **JJ** synchronised movement on the dance floor. The Tiller Girls are the spectacle, but psytrance is the festival. It's like that thing Rousseau said: 'The theatre is to the festival what totalitarianism is to democracy.' So, the theatre is a space of hierarchical visuality—we are there to see and also to be seen, of course. But the festival is more fluid, and you can move wherever you want at any given moment, and there's an omni-visuality, in terms of the body and what it chooses to see from moment to moment. In a lot of ways, this is the difference between cinema and video art: in a gallery space, we can look at a video, and come in and out of that environment at any given moment. We choose whether or not to comply, and stay throughout its duration. Whereas, in a cinema, we're pretty much required to sit in a fixed position and look.

So, in a way, the dance floor and video art have these modes of resistance towards the spectacle within them. (Laughing) Not a massive mode of resistance, but there is a temporality of resistance within video art and the elective experience of dance.

DG With all that in mind, I'd like to ask you about your film, *Zarathustra* (2008). It seems to be pervaded by spectral presences, in the same way that *The Spectre and the Sphere* (2008) is haunted by the ghost of communism. In *Zarathustra*, the theme tune for *2001: A Space Odyssey* is played by the Artane Boys Band in a derelict Ballymun swimming pool. It's as though the sci-fi film's futurism is twinned with the sixties' optimism surrounding the launch of the ill-fated Ballymun housing estate. Perhaps the meeting of the militaristic nostalgia with the softer leisure activity of swimming evokes your scrambling together of Meyerholdian constructivist spectacle and the capitalist spectacle of Busby Berkeley's films. It seems sad and faintly ridiculous that this bored-looking boys band—whose membership is now half female—is playing a thrustingly futuristic tune in a monument to failed capitalism—an empty swimming pool. The militarist aspect suggests to me the cultural poverty of a society that rehabilitates war into a leisure pursuit. Also, there's the idea that women are being co-opted into a militaristic mentality, rather than steering men towards more enlightened options. We might wonder if we should not be encouraging children towards more self-realising pastimes, such as learning why war happens. The Orwellian idea that wars are fought by the ruling classes against their own lower orders also seems to surface. As regards the Nietzschean title of your film, could the Übermensch (or the 'Supermen') here be the architects of public policy who instigated the Ballymun housing estate? Supermen with feet of clay.

JJ That's a really nice way of speaking about the work. I didn't make the connection before between the formation of a military band and the Meyerholdian constructivist thing, but, yeah, it makes sense, for sure. That work is about my wanting to mark that space in some way, and create a kind of focus on the space through sounds and through incident. It was almost a kind of impossible and bizarre moment with this drab, drained-out swimming pool. It has fallen into decay, and a kind of failure, and because of that failure, it can now be a stage for another event. So, in a way, my film is a critique of the collapse of the utopian housing project, but it's also asking 'What can be recuperated from that? How can you change the meaning of this failure, and turn it into a space for some other cultural activity?' So I don't think it's a deeply cynical work.

There's an idea of the spectre of the future: [Richard Strauss'] *Zarathustra* song from Kubrick's film could be the soundtrack for a future utopia that could be found among the bones of the failures of the past. So I feel my film can be both things at once: it can speak of collapse, and simultaneously suggest the building of something positive on the site of previous failure. The young people represent a sense of renewal and optimism for me, too, even though uniforms are associated with conformity. I think the fact that they have drifted away from being a boy's band, and they now have girls in their ranks too, speaks of a potential for optimism—that you can take historical meanings and shift them. I feel that *Zarathustra* is the most cheerful artwork I've done! What you say about it is very articulate and really interesting, but I think it's a happy artwork about how new possibilities can be salvaged from devastating collapse.

The film is an exploration of what we accept as historical content, but it's also asking: 'What can future generations do with what we discard, and what we don't accord meaning to?' It's a very surreal work in that, if this were a functioning swimming pool what I have filmed could never happen. And their uniforms are blue, and there's an allusion towards whether there's a sense of a creation of a doubling of a space of the past and the present. As you first move through the space with the camera, there's a feeling of: 'Are we trying to find an active swimming pool? Are we going to turn the corner and see people jumping into a pool? Is it between two corners?'

DG That's a bit reminiscent of *The Struggle Against Ourselves*—the doubling aspect—where the first part shows a rather gruelling, utilitarian Meyerholdian workshop, and the second features a contrastingly graceful dream sequence.

JJ Yes, that's a quite simple structure that I use in my work. It's about using the space of the film to double the sense of time. So this moment of quite utilitarian, quotidian activity of processing knowledge and trying to inhabit that within your body in the first part of the film can then allude to another time when that can be a dream sequence, or it could be part of your subconscious, or it could be from another historical moment. It could be something that never happened, physically, in what we consider the real world, but happens in a dream space.

DG It's akin to the Freudian idea of the Dreamwork, how our unconscious puts our dreams into metaphorical code so that we're not awoken by disturbing content.

JJ I was obsessed with dream sequences in films when I was growing up. When I first wanted to make films, it really clicked with me that dream sequences are this incredible conduit between naturalist representation and the psychoanalytical, dreaming sense of: 'Is this really happening?' And I think that's why I have such a deep commitment to film—the possibility of exploring the nature of what passes for reality.

DG In *The Predicament of Man* (2010), images of twentieth/twenty-first century civilisation flash onto the screen—almost like a nod to subliminal advertising—while the camera pans languidly across the arid landscape of an opal mine in Cobber Pedy, Australia. It looks like the end of the world. Are you drawing attention to the over-mining of the earth's resources, and the attendant surfeit of images in late capitalist society? We de(p)lete the real environment and make images for a populace divorced from the real. So we end up with a hyperreal environment. As when a council demolishes a park to make a road full of 'desirable residences' and…

JJ Names the road after the park!

DG Yeah, calls the new road 'Park Way' in non-ironic commemoration of what they have just destroyed. *The Predicament of Man* seems to me like Jean Baudrillard channelling Shelley's *Ozymandias*. That line, 'Look on my works, ye mighty, and despair!' flits through my mind every time I see that film.

JJ The way that work came about is so strange that there's not one way of describing it. That's one of the shortest films I've made, but I actually spent nine months making it. *The Predicament of Man* actually came from writing, when I was living in New York. I'd made the film: I'd shot the 15 mil pan of the desert in Australia, but I knew that I wanted to do something with it, and I couldn't really figure out what it was. I knew I had to have it sit in the studio, until I found out what would happen with it. So I just began a writing process. I started to write this really strange novel in New York in 2009/2010, and I would write every day for eight hours. After sitting and writing for that long, I'd really think about what I was doing with my work. Up to this point, so much of my work had been so image-based—and based upon my thinking about the image as a material and source—that I really wanted to pull back from the visual. So the writing for eight hours a day was a narrative drawing process, and after a day of stream-of-consciousness writing, I would try to structure a story. I ended up writing a story about a man who disappears. He goes to live with an archivist, who discovers this transformational space, and they both disappear down this wormhole of historical material. So I was really thinking about how you can disappear into the image, and be cognitively obliterated by such a rapid-paced visual culture—thinking about the effect this has upon human intimacy. It touches upon the exponential rise of the image. At this moment in history, we are able to process more images than ever before, and what does that do to us at a deeper, biological level? So I'm marking that monumental shift into hyperreality.

So it's not a predominantly pessimistic piece? **DG**

No, again, I don't feel I'm presenting a nightmarish situation, **JJ** and I wanted the [quite soothing] music I used in the film to signal that. At the time, I was very obsessed with Bruegel paintings, and I was thinking about that scene in *Solaris*, where they had the Pieter Bruegel the Elder painting, *The Hunters in the Snow*. It becomes this moment that ruptures the situation that they're in, and there's this sense of nostalgia within the image. It's so emotional when you see that Bruegel painting, and, even though there's a lot of images in *The Predicament of Man*, I spent a long time carefully choosing each image. I wanted it to be evocative in the same way that the Bruegel scene in *Solaris* is. That's why it took nine months to make the film.

The schism between the agricultural life of regional Ireland **DG** and the modernity of Dublin is very striking, and perhaps this fissure is displaced in your film and surfaces as the juxtaposition between an ancient Australian landscape and multiple flash images of modern life. I wonder if that's an oblique way for you to process the sensory onslaught of modern life—again, in a similar way to the Freudian Dreamwork? Even as your work is intensely modern and metropolitan, it seems to signal your concern about contemporary glibness. The novel you were talking about writing seems to dovetail with such ideas.

JJ One of the things that was a recurrent theme in that book was the symbolism of the elephant. I had been reading José Saramago, as well. I'm quite interested in strange ideas, like how elephants can be seen as a monument to the brutality of some aspects of modernity. In *The Predicament of Man*, there's about fifty images of elephants, so that's one of the sub-texts within the film. There are a lot of things within my films that become part of the thinking, conceptually, but they aren't always front-loaded. But, when I was living in New York, I was really interested in the story of Topsy the elephant [the animal lived in Coney Island, and was killed by poisoning and electrocution by her allegedly abusive owners on account of her reported aggression. This unedifying spectacle was overseen by Thomas Edison in 1903]. She had been electrocuted by Edison, as a way of showing the power of his version of electricity. It was the moment that he trumped his competitor, Nikola Tesla, and Edison became the go-to guy for electricity. And it was because of the assassination of this tiny rogue elephant in Coney Island that the twentieth century in America looks the way it does.

So, there are a lot of things that are interesting to me that may indeed stem from my being Irish and having the opportunity to travel. I get a lot of inspiration when I'm outside of Ireland. When I went to Seoul, it really turned a light on in my head about Ireland, and a lot of the preparatory research for my film, *The Other North* (2013), was made in my hotel room. I got the direction of the work in Seoul, and then came back to Ireland and accessed the archival materials I needed to mould the work.

Could you say more about how *The Other North* came about? **DG**

I've never really spoken about this before, but there's a **JJ** sense of being an artist in the world that is a little cheesy and bourgeois, you know. You can come from a working class background, and you can even be Irish, but it's still a bit cheesy and bourgeois. Especially, once you're flying around the world, staying in hotels, and being brought out to launches, and so on. You're a bit of a show pony, in a lot of ways, even though you have to work pretty fucking hard. So that part of the gig makes you feel a little bit uneasy, especially when you've been invited somewhere to make a work.

I was talking to a lot of artists when I was commissioned to make a work in Seoul, and people were very fascinated by the idea of being commissioned to make a film there: what would you do, as an Irish person? I felt really resistant to making a film about Korea, because I thought: 'What right do I have to make a work about somewhere I don't really have a context for?' So I wanted to deal with the responsibility of making a film about somewhere else by bringing a lot of my own historical baggage to the project—baggage that I'd never even looked at before. It had always been in my peripheral field of vision, but I was never in the position of knowing how I could find a lens to look at my own history. I mean, growing up in Ireland, you would turn the television on at six o' clock at night, and Gerry Adams would be played by an actor; there was this sense, immediately—when you're growing up and you're starting to contemplate the world—that there's something staged and surreal about what is being presented to the viewing public as 'real life'. So, growing up with these actors providing the voices for real people, it embedded the idea in me that the media is a stage—that there's an aspect of fiction and performance to this medium that purports to be transmitting facts. So, I suppose, when I went to Korea, it heightened and caused a resurgence of those feelings.

Also, I'm not from Korea, and I'm not from Northern Ireland either, so it's about finding a way to look at both of these things through a filter of mutual estrangement. And, being in Seoul, there's a sense that people really feel that a prosperous, happy future is possible and maybe they blank out the north of their country, which is how I felt growing up during the Celtic Tiger. The attitude was: 'Of course, it's leading to this inevitable future that's going to be full of progress, prosperity and wonderful things'—which turned out not to be true. So there was a sense of ignoring what was happening in the north of Ireland, because you were in this dream-like bubble of affluence, and you didn't have to think about the north. The north was a million miles away. This is how Seoulites feel about north Korea, in a lot of ways. Even when these moments of crisis came along, you'd talk to people on the streets of Seoul on Monday morning, and they would say: 'It happens! It will be fine.' So there's that feeling of the distance that such a massive difference in circumstances can make. As a result of that, I was really thinking about how the details of the conflict in Northern Ireland in the seventies could awake dormant aspects of the political consciousness now in Korea. I worked intensely with people there: a film maker, a psychologist, and lots of people who were really embedded in the academic and political thinking about modern Korea.

DG Did you encounter any resistance from northern Irish people of the 'what right does a 'blow-in' have to take on such a charged part of our history' variety? It's human nature to be territorial about historical topics as well as land masses, after all.

JJ I thought of it in the opposite way. In a lot of ways, the reason I made the film is because I'm not from the North, and the aim was to create a work about universal human politics. It's actually about how we form conflict with other human beings—how we are in the world with each other. So, if somebody from the Falls Road is being played by a Korean soap opera actor, that's how the viewer can see that it's not just about someone from the Falls Road and their position in the world—it's a position that anybody can empathise with and understand. So actually extracting it from place, and extracting it from specific national identity is a way that we can see this crisis as a human experience.

So you're saying that the fact that the Troubles were not part of your direct experience allowed you to conceive of the sectarian divide in universal human terms? **DG**

It freed me, in a lot of ways. I invited Eamonn McCann [the Derry-based author, journalist and political activist] to come to a screening of the work and speak with me about it. I was very anxious about him seeing the film. You know, he'd be quite an embedded person within northern Irish politics for the last forty years, in terms of the Saville inquiry and his political activism. So it was quite nerve-wracking for me to invite him to watch the film, knowing that he was going to be speaking with me publicly, after having just seen the work. I was very open to any kind of criticism: if people were really angry about the work, I really wanted to expose the film to critical conflict. After all, it's a film. It's not as if I'm going out and doing something that's going to interrupt things and fuck people's lives up. They watch a film, and if it triggers feelings of hatred or empathy, at least the work has instigated a debate. But he actually really, really liked the work and said that it was very interesting to see the situation that he was so used to being defamiliarised in that way. He was talking about how he was so used to a certain kind of visual representation of that political conflict—like the paintings on the walls in Derry—and, I guess, for him to see it within a different cultural context moved it into a kind of dream sequence. **JJ**

Again, I'd say that this type of dream sequence contains some truth within the dream that's more powerful than the truth that's in the so-called 'real.' It was about seeing the entire history of the Troubles anew through this very particular kind of estrangement. That kind of almost Brechtian alienation technique. And when the work was shown in Korea, there was the same response to it, because the type of anxieties humans feel about 'the other' are universal. That's why I think the Rogerian psychotherapy script was a really great lens through which to view both big political history and the personal concerns within it. So you get verbatim conversations with a woman who had two kids who kept getting picked up by the British police, and they were joining the IRA. She's telling this very human story of the experience of actually being a mother within a massive civil crisis and a war zone. It's not about the British police, it's about being a mother and how do you protect your children in the world. What kind of agency do you have when the personal is destabilised by wider social forces? These are the kind of questions that Bertolt Brecht and Siegfried Kracauer ask in their work.

DG What's your take on the way films distort history by sentimentality, oversimplification and anachronism? For example, in Shane Meadows' film, *This Is England* (2006), we are offered an anodyne rehashing of David Leland's gritty TV film, *Made In England* (1982), which depicts the life of a delinquent skinhead in eighties' England. The newer film featured jolting anachronisms, such as the use of Antipodean/American high rise terminals (or 'uptalk'), something that was not in evidence in the era depicted. Also, a skinhead gang leader in the Meadows film was apt to hug distressed gang members, which was highly unfeasible and seemed like a clumsy attempt to enlist the audience's empathy.

Given these aspects of mainstream film, how do you feel about the idea that film is an inferior art form, when compared with theatre, for instance?

JJ I don't really think that it is. I think it's got to do with how we remember and how there are ways of re-experiencing the past. And I think that a lot of the strategies of emotionalising or sentimentalising representations of the past are kind of useful as well, in terms of giving emotional structure to a viewer in order for them to be able to enter into the dynamic that's happening. If you think of that Ken Loach film, *The Wind That Shakes The Barley*, it could be argued to be over-sentimentalising the experience of gun-running by members of the IRA, but there is a necessity to kind of allow for that emotional representation of the past. You can have a stoic singularity about how we describe the past, but I don't think it should be either/or. I think it's sometimes quite useful to be able to use emotion, and to use cinema as a space for creating empathetic representations of people within a moment of time that we're not experiencing. Maybe their struggles will resonate with us.

I mean, E.P. Thompson's *The Making of the English Working Class* is an incredibly emotional representation of British working-class consciousness, through the centuries. You could say that the book is sentimental in how it talks about the minutiae of daily life, and what it's like to have to talk about trouble at Old Mill. So sentimentality is not confined to cinema: it's a cynical position to say that all film is marred by sentimentality, because some films utilise such emotions without craft. It's possible to use the strategy of melodrama in ways that can be very politically empowering.

DG But comparing a work of humanist social history with a mainstream film is not comparing like with like. I agree that melodrama can generate empathy, but do you not think that you're conflating the idea of being an artist who sifts through popular culture for hidden meanings with a more typical punter who goes down the multiplex for a fairly passive entertainment experience? A lot of people won't have gone to college, so don't have access to the discourse that you apply to film.

JJ I kind of trust people's instinct about cinema. We grow up watching films, and you can talk to anybody about cinema, and pretty much everybody will have something interesting to say about it, because it's a very direct experience. It's very accessible, in a lot of ways. I mean, I went to see a film in a multiplex the other day. It was pretty boring, but there were definitely levels of readability in it that were stimulating, and it was only ninety minutes of my life. I still think that the multiplex can be a space where interesting ideas can form. Obviously, those ideas need to be held within a holistic understanding of other cultural things that are happening in the world, but the multiplex is definitely part of our cultural staple diet. I mean, Steve McQueen's new film, *12 Years A Slave*, is a great example of how the multiplex can really be mobilised to make very complex arguments about history. Obviously, he's worked through a video art and art practice for the last fifteen or twenty years, and moved into the multiplex because it's a way of spreading his ideas more widely. And you could argue that to go from *Hunger* to this new film is a kind of Hollywood leap, and perhaps there might have had to have been compromises in terms of the storytelling not being as obscure or as oblique as he was allowed to be within the field of video art. But the audience is so much wider and the film has to resonate with people at various different levels. I would still have a lot of optimism about the potential of the multiplex film.

DG In the final paragraph of the Clara Kim interview about *The Struggle Against Ourselves*, you say the following: 'I think there is an interesting dynamic between socialist realism as a kind of self-heroism of the masses and postmodernism, where the consumer appears as the central locus of power, but has no actual power at all. We are part of the Spectacle, but have no control over it.'

Is there a sense in which your work is attempting to draw attention to—and even dismantle—the Spectacle? Is there a positive and optimistic sense of your wanting to return agency and autonomy to disenfranchised people? This is the feeling I got from *12 Angry Films*, which was influenced by Augusta Boal's *Theatre of the Oppressed*. Your film seems concerned to take the 'non-places' that the French anthropologist, Marc Augé writes about, and re-humanise them into places where people feel validated, rather than diminished, as individuals.

JJ That idea of people being validated and not diminished by places like the drive-in environment of *12 Angry Films* resonates with me. One of my commitments to cinema is that I feel fundamentally that it's a space where we can gather to be part of a viewership. The drive-in was always a very exciting place for me, thinking about the potential it had to undo the American Dream of the fifties, which was to have this perfect suburban house and car while the Cold War was going on, and there was this fear of communism. But, even within that, the kind of popular culture encounter that was set up by drive-ins had a heterotopic element in that you had privacy sitting in your car, away from the gaze of authority, and you could begin to speak. And, also, because of the privacy afforded by the car, the drive-in was one of the first racially de-segregated spaces in American culture. So I genuinely feel that there's always some kind of heterotopic element within the spectacle. It will always have this grain of possibility for another way of encountering it. There is always some kind of wormhole embedded within it that deconstructs the dominant rationale for its existence. It's just a question of finding it.

Thornback Ray
Desmond Hogan

'And what do you want the *Complete Grimm Fairytales* for, if you don't mind me asking?' the suburban librarian, in a low-cut sweater, with horizontal strawberry stripes, which left one arm bare, beside a Tucan twister plant (twisted and intertangled stem trunk), asked me as if she was thinking of calling the Guards.

The Scottish fiddler and composer Niel Gow, who played for Prince Charlie at Dunkeld on his march south to Edinburgh, whose tune 'The Lass o' Gowrie' Robbie Burns used as setting for 'Address To The Woodlark', when asked how he managed the long road home from Perth to Inver after a ball, said it wasn't the length of the road he minded but the breadth of it. He gave the distance as ten Scotch miles.

I don't know why I must retrace this lonely, lonely road out of Ireland, but I must. I must find this Icarus with a life sentence.

The stories the House Father (Social Worker) read to the boy were of journeys: *The Wonderful Adventures* of Nils Holsgersson—a little boy turned into an elf and borne on a goose's back; *The Snow Queen*—Gerda who journeyed, with nothing to protect her but the Lord's Prayer, to the palace of the Snow Queen to find her lost brother Kay; *The Little Mermaid*—a mermaid who forfeited her mermaid's tail and her tongue and journeyed to land to find the Prince she'd fallen in love with; *The Wild Swans*—Eliza carried by the eleven swans who'd been her brothers, who'd written with diamond pencils on slates of gold, praying to protect herself against naked lamias who clawed open fresh graves, snatched up corpses and devoured the flesh as she was to collect the nettles she would weave to restore her brothers to permanently human form; *Thumbelina*—snatched from the imminence of a marriage to mole by a swallow she'd revived from a state of death and borne to a land of blue and green grapes, lemons and oranges, myrtles and balsams; Thumbling carried in a horse's ear, a cow's belly, a wolf's paunch; Aladdin borne through the air by the Slave of the Lamp to a hammam made of jade, transparent alabaster, with pools of rose, carnelian and white coral, ornamentation of large emeralds, where he was massaged by young men of girl-beauty, washed with musk-scented rose water, given a sherbet of musk and snow and summer flower; *Dracula*—the vampire Lucy Westenra trails children. Would the Social Worker have brought the boy to St. Michan's and showed him the four mummified nuns and the mummified cat chasing a rat in the organ—one of the inspirations for Dracula?

To write with a diamond pencil on a slate of gold!

The Social Worker's writing was stilted, awkward, tilted to left, low self-esteem betrayed.

In prison one is cut off from history. One is cut off from source. Your existence becomes scatological. It becomes surcrease. One is robbed of imagination and if any signs of imagination remain—like *tachiste* (blotted colour) graffiti on the cell wall—you are driven into more extreme isolation. Like a mountain goat into a crevice.

The only option that remains is to end your existence with a garment ligature.

But the image, the reflection of the child remains to the end, Christopher (Christ-bearer)—Reprobus—carrying the child across the river, a mermaid, holding up her mirror, looking on.

When Christopher planted his staff by the side of the river after bearing the child, flowers and dates sprung from it.

When he was being tried in Edinburgh, January 1978, the Social Worker remembered posies of goat's rue and lad's love (old man, southernwood)—dull yellow flowers that don't come in cool summers—were placed in court once to protect against jail fever from prisoners.

Ashes of lad's love mixed with salad oil for baldness or beard regeneration. Its kindred flower mugwort planted beside roads by Roman soldiers—to put in their sandals on long marches. Perhaps that's why mugwort still grows by waysides.

Near Glenochil Prison mugwort grows by the ruins of the Antonine Wall, ordered by the Roman Emperor Antoninus Pius.

In Victorian times *artemisia abrotanum* was symbolic of love between a man and a boy.

Because of love of a boy, a life sentence in Glenochil, Clackmannanshire—the smallest county—a male long-term prison.

Saint Begnet of Dalkey, who'd been betrothed to the son of the King of Norway, had made her way to Clackmannanshire from Cumberland and founded a chapel.

An angel had given her a bracelet in Ireland marked with the sign of the cross, as a symbol of her vocation, and by the twelfth century accusers and accused were asked to swear their testimony on the bracelet:

You've got to hold on to the dream no matter what. If you don't have the dream you have nothing. They don't understand. We lived in a dream for centuries; I killed to keep the dream.

Glenochil—a veto on your instincts, on your existence, on memory, the river in you.

The Cookstown and the Dargle Rivers met in Enniskerry, County Wicklow, where the boy scouts go. The head bottle washer of the scouts live nearby. The boy scouts would put black shoe polish on a tenderfoot's balls as initiation.

It was mostly Irishmen, their lodging separated from Scottish workers, who built the Caledonian (Edinburgh, Glasgow, Carlisle) and North British (Edinburgh-Berwick) lines. The Forbes family of Callendar House, where the marriage agreement between Mary Stuart and the French Dauphin was signed, did not wish to look on a canal, so in 1822 the Union Canal, longest canal tunnel in Scotland, was cut through by Irishmen, many of whom were killed by rocks.

New Publications section of *Edinburgh Annual Register* for 1813 cites 'Glenochil', a descriptive poem by James Kennedy in two volumes.

Robbie Burns, who was knighted in Clackmannanshire with the two-handed sword of Robert Bruce, wrote his last poem about the River Devon near Glenochil Prison.

'Crystal Devon, winding Devon...'

The River Devon rises behind Ben Cleuch, highest peak in the Ochil Hills, which you can see from the north side of Glenochil Prison, and joins the River Forth (five and a quarter miles away as the crow flies) but takes over thirty miles.

The Ochil Hills as you can see them from the north side of Glenochil Prison have slashed deep ravines, steep gorges, sides swooping without foothills directly to flats as a consequence of the Ochil fault which plunges thousands of feet below the silted up flood plain.

Mary Queen of Scots attended a wedding in 1563 in Castle Campbell on those southern facing slopes and John Knox administered the sacrament of the Lord's Supper on the grassy slopes between castle and cliff.

'Pity me, Kinsmen, for the sake of Jesus Christ, who pitied all the world,' Mary Stuart's young husband Lord Henry Darnley cried as he was strangled outside Edinburgh, naked but for a nightgown.

Murderers with life sentences were on the third floor of A Block in Glenochil, sexual offenders on the first floor of A Block. Sexual offenders' windows were blacked out. They were known as The Beasts. Bags of excrement and urine were thrown at them from B Block and C Block.

There was a tropical fish tank online sentence floor—leopard catfish, suckermouth catfish, salt and pepper catfish, pineapple pleco, orange cheeked pleco, and a corydoras, black dwarf corydoras.

Lifers have nothing to prove. They just want to get on with life sentence.

The Prison Chef had previously been employed in the Dorchester—a four star hotel.

There were three metal gates between educational building and the Blocks to deter metal objects. You could learn hairdressing in the educational building. You could learn engineering, tap and dye, iron casting.

The adjoining coalboard offices were turned into junior offender cells.

One hour visits were allowed.

There was a man in Glenochil who made fudge in the microwave from Bounty Bars, sweetened condensed milk, Nesquik milkshakes.

Prison workers, trained in mouth-to-mouth resuscitation, regularly found bodies.

Glenochil has the seventh highest suicide rate in Scotland.

'If they get pipes out they can hang themselves from them, can electrocute themselves with wires.'

They could hang themselves with electric wires, aluminium wires, aluminium piping, metal cages.

Beds were bolted to the floor but if they could get them up they could hang themselves from them.

They could hang themselves from low bar cells if they pulled their legs up.

There were searchlights in Glenochil prison yard.

'Being gay was a terrible thing in Glenochil. No maturation. No development.'

> *'I swear by the Blessed Trinitie*
> *I have no wife, no children, I,*
> *Nor dwelling at home in merrie Scotland.'*

The boy had the probation genitals of a nine year old, like a butterfly orchid.

Scorched by bath water in an Edinburgh hotel, opposite Waverley Station, his body, found on the Feast of Giovanni Bernadone, Saint Francis of Assisi, looked like a common spotted orchid white as the top of the Himalayas.

'It was just horseplay,' the Social Worker, who was found with sixty-nine tablets, told the police.

The Queen had asked a huntsman to kill Snow White and bring back her lung and liver. Snow White's coffin had been made of transparent glass.

In Mount Jerome Cemetery, where the boy was buried in Saint Luke's summer, the thinnest fox lives.

It was believed in Ireland a child would die if raven's eggs, pale blue to pale green, were stolen. A raven lives in the Scotch pine in the cemetery—nest a cup of dried grass, moss, lined with rabbit fur.

Buzzards pass from Wales, hovering over the cemetery, miaowing like a cat, mobbed by jackdaws who try to settle their tail.

A family of sparrowhawks live in an abandoned crow's nest in poplars by the River Poddle in the cemetery.

Saint Charles of Mount Argus lived nearby, who cried during the Sacred Passion and who'd cured a boy of blindness, the boy later becoming a Carmelite priest.

A Russian youth stokes the ashes in the crematorium now.

Did the funeral party—mother, mother's mother, mother's sister—stand among the poppies with white beards by the Grand Canal and watch an otter crunch an eel?

Reflections in Snow White's transparent coffin. Inner Dublin Streets.

The Roma Café in Dorset Street which sold thornback ray—humpy ray you ate, off the bone.

A lemon, lighted up fish with scarlet arrow, flickering on and off, on his back, pointing the way into the chipper.

A boy in scarlet jersey suddenly veering vertically across the road in disregard of the traffic, onto the opposite pavement, like a cardinal bird let loose in these parts.

Sean McDermott Street in snow, like L.S. Lowry's paintings of Salford, ensembles of tiny figures adrift, muted, made a joke of against the Titan blocks of flats.

A woman wheeling a pram full of king-size Twix bars.

Skinheads with baby bottom haircuts.

Youths in hipster jeans with Mick Jagger haircuts.

Youths in diamond pattern jerseys with Eric Burdon and the Animals haircuts—plastic, side-swept quiffs.

Pot belly stove in an orphanage and a picture of Mary on the wall, who looks as if she's had a ghetto nervous breakdown, pointing to her heart.

To find your way home with white pebbles that glitter in the moonlight like coins. A duck individually ferried Hänsel and Gretel across an expanse of water on their final journey home.

The deepest and loneliest part of the wood where a white bird brings you to a house whose walls are made of gingerbread, roof of cake, windows pure sugar.

The boy's family—mother, grandmother, mother's partner—considered they were having a sexual relationship. Those in authority tried to separate them. What's sexual at seven, eight, nine? Sleeping naked together, touching, fondling?

When someone has had a sexual relationship at six they may later in life seek sexual relations with six year olds. A man in their part of Dublin—where, when a medical school was turned into a national school, barefoot boys played hurling with human bones and skulls, where Matt Talbot ate dry bread, drank cocoa without milk or sugar, slept on a plank with a wooden plank for a pillow—joined the British Foreign Services and sought child prostitutes in Asian cities. When someone has had a sexual experience at six they may later in life like looking at photographs of nude six year olds—red smartie penis on small ball of genitals.

A birch tree grows outside St Giles Cathedral, ragwort and fleabane by steps leading to the castle.

The Royal British Hotel opposite Waverley Station—Scottish baronial turret, Dutch windows, dormer windows.

Disney shop underneath it now.

There were mobile statuettes on the top ledge, moving theatricals. The statuette of Pinocchio fell apart on the ledge and became dangerous and had to be removed. Bits of it could have fallen on customers.

We have a cowslip-blonde Alice in Wonderland with the Cheshire Cat, the Mad Hatter in what looks like a mock football supporters' hat, samovar beside him with Russian flowers on it, the March Hare with cake; the Little Mermaid with 1940's roll top, lilac bra, tail which looks like single green leggings, Flounder the Fish; Dumbo the Flying Elephant with his one friend, Timothy the Mouse, in brimmed hat; the house of Geppetto, Pinocchio's maker; six brooms from Fantasia; Pluto, Minnie Mouse in elbow and strawberry polka dot dress with cup sleeves, using a vintage camera; a smaller Minnie Mouse in red and white polka dot with matching ribbons; Mickey Mouse in very short shorts with two white eyes on each of them which could be taken to have a sexual meaning.

When you wake or are woken at night you try to hold something the way the Little Mermaid held the drowning Prince, brought him to shore, saved his life. You try to bring something to shore. You try to salvage something.

Your train journey to Edinburgh was theirs, past sea-houses, Saint Cuthbert Island where the saint lived as a hermit, Inner Farne Island where Saint Aidan from Galway would spend Lent, where Saint Cuthbert lived in solitude and died. The Farne Islands are a sanctuary for birds and seals now.

On the main door of Durham Cathedral where Saint Cuthbert is buried is the Sanctuary Knocker—tongue of a demon with holes as eyes, flews on his face, dog's ears aureole of sunrays.

Knock it if you murdered someone and you get thirty-seven days sanctuary within the cathedral and a possible chance to flee the country.

> *'O spare my life! O spare my life!*
> *O spare my life!' said he;*

> *'If ever I live to be a young man,
> I'll do a good chare for thee.'*

I feel I am the one running away from Ireland with this boy—running away from ignorance, Medievalism, chasing some truth.

There's no truth in the land the man and the boy are fleeing.

It's a land of lies.

Victorian *béguinage* architecture—tower rooms, dormer windows, turrets, iron crosses with circles in the centre; titanium and ichorous statues of the Sacred Heart; spring heather and *hebe*; larch trees, yew trees.

Hebe, goddess of youth, Ganymeda her other name, but it was Ganymede who was chosen here.

I ask where the Child Care Centre was.

'Was that where all the abuse was?'

An avenue of lime trees (*crann teile*) with trunks covered in ivy as if to hide some shame.

National Park lodge-house type apartments with bird tables outside.

The name of the house has been changed to Hawthorn.

Embassy of the Islamic Republic of Iran nearby, St. Andrew's Presbyterian Church, St. Philip and St. James Church of Ireland with its pines, firs, arbutus.

'Are you treasure hunting?'

There was no Aladdin's cave like that boy.

Face like a wren's egg in a lost property department, white, delicately speckled reddish.

The red of the fox against the yellow of the winter dunes;

his hair was like that. Eyes like the dog violets sprinkled in them emerald-green dune moss.

In his smile was a journey on a goose's back, in the clutch of eleven swans, in the clutch of the Slave of the Lamp, on a swallow's back, with his feet on the swallow's outspread wings bound by a girdle to one of the swallow's strangest feathers.

Beechwood Road, Ranelagh, Leenane No. 18—Cambridge blue door Yukon No. 15—glass door. Nanvilla No. 13—Staffordshire terriers in transom. 12—pale, too pale terracotta. Roundel mosaic print lawn pathway. Chinese puzzle hedges. Claret and yellow glass windows at back of house.

Beechwood Road—pampas grass, sumac trees, lots of schoolboys in blue the same colour as the door of No. 18. The House Father, the Social Worker, lived in No. 12.

1977. The lonely year. The year of leaving. The year 364 heads of Old Testament Kings, decapitated on the facade of Notre Dame in Paris during the Revolution, were found when they were digging the foundations of a bank in Paris.

The year or trying. Of running away. Of wanting to be lover to a boy-child.

Close by the Hiberno-Romanesque Church of the Holy Name in Albany Road where the Social Worker faithfully attended mass.

Did the Social Worker have zealot's features, some hurt, some deprivation from childhood challenging you? Was he a culchie? (From the country.) He had one previous conviction though it's not stated what for. Did he and the boy sleep in the same bed in flight? Did the boy wear blue pajamas with a pattern of soccer balls?

Did the Social Worker sing lullabies to the boy—*The October winds lament Around the castle of Dromore... Clan Eoan's wild banshee'*—as a nurse used to sing *Marlborough s'en va-t-en guerre* (Marlborough has left for the war), composed the night after the Battle of Malplaquet 1709, to Marie Antoinette's children as a lullaby?

Did the Social Worker have dark algal pubic hair like the hair the Little Mermaid's sister cut off so they could get a knife from the sea-witch which when stuck in the Prince's heart would bring warm blood which would restore the Little Mermaid's fish-tail?

In the Ranelagh Takeaway as it begins to snow there's a small boy with a flamingo band running over top of head and down back of it, tall, older brother in habit-brown tracksuit.

Love is a stranger in Dublin. Love belongs to another decade.

Truth is another time, another another country.

'I'll get you a cup of tea, one slice of toast, one sausage in Bewley's,' I once heard a small pawky boy with pink freckles like sweet pea say to an unwhetted Croppy from Wicklow or Wexford on Grafton Street.

A decade when Tattens—Large Coffee (Kathleen Toomey), ashy bouffant, geranium lipstick, with Mount Merrion accent, from a part of Wicklow with stubborn homesteads, mad cows, rams with Methuselah beards, used jog, carnation in lapel, with a large coffee and a Mary cake—biscuit base, chocolate filling, almond icing, mint embossments—to have her pet customers in Bewley's Grafton Street, so eager was she to deliver them.

Tattens started her workday with a prayer in Clarendon Street Church.

Used holiday with young waitresses in Gran Canaria, Lanzarote, Tenerife, dress up in her evenings there in white cotton blouses, flower-printed collarless blouses, white flower-printed cotton dresses, white straw hats, blue leather shoes, bead necklaces and earrings and chat in red hotel lobbies to Guanches boys—descendants of the blonde-haired people who'd originally lived on the Canaries.

Mayerling was a big hit in Dublin then, Rudolf, Archduke and Crown Prince of Austria, who committed joint suicide in a hunting lodge in Mayerling, fifteen miles south west of Vienna, with his seventeen-year-old cousin, the Baroness Maria Vetsera, on the morning of January 30 1889.

So was Elvira Madigan about the twenty-one-year-old German-born circus acrobat, her step father John Madigan the circus owner, who was shot by thirty-four-year-old Swedish Cavalry Lieutenant Sixten Sparre in the forest of Neorreskov on the Danish Island of Tåsinge, with his service revolver, after they'd made love for the last time in Renoir haze on July 1 1889, he then ending his own life in a similar manner.

> *'Danced she on a tightrope lightly,*
> *Glad as the skylark in the sky.'*

Cleopatra was frequently recalled to Dublin in which Elizabeth Taylor is borne into Rome on a Sphinx and in which she commits suicide with an aureus—cobra—bite, following Richard Burton's suicide as Anthony in the same month, August 30 BC.

You frequently found yourself looking at a poster for *Cleopatra* with Rex Harrison as Caesar gazing at enthroned Cleopatra like a lascivious vicar.

Grallatorial boys—long legged like the football teams of herons—who stalk the water edge—would wander the dunes of North Bull Island then seeking sexual pick ups. Milkshake coloured bodies. They used soother cream—antiseptic lotion—or white cream for scabies for suntan lotion. They'd exchange sex for Carroll's cigarettes or Lemons sweets. Brylcreem. Toothpaste. Toothbrushes.

They assessed clients the way the foxes who live in the dunes assessed intruders.

The fox knows how to offset himself against harebells because it is photogenic.

A fox had got into Dublin Zoo looking for small creatures and a polar bear ate him.

To sool the rabbits on Bull Island. They used to put den nets for the hares on Bull Island, have greyhounds chase them. They would put down nets in the dunes the way trinkermen would put down trink-nets—fixed nets in the Thames in Elizabethan times. They'd block off rabbit holes, pin nets down, send ferrets in after rabbits.

Winter evenings when the sunset looked like a sleeping fox and the dunes were fox-coloured.

The man and the boy ran away in September, month of the fox, month of the harebell.

'She had an alcoholic husband who died. The Social Worker wished to foster the child. The authorities tried to separate them. Decided to run away with the boy. He was affiliated to some Christian Brothers.

It was a culture, an otherness with the Christian Brothers. They had a hard life. The Church treated them badly.

It was an attraction to innocence, by taking innocence you destroyed it, possessed it.

He had a burden of otherness. He ran away with the boy and murdered him in this otherness.

It's also about control. You can control. End the life of a nine-year-old boy.'

Gerald Griffin from Pallaskenry, County Limerick—mutton chop locks, widow's peak, girl's brows and mouth—given to high talk, turned his back on his literary success at the age of thirty-five in 1838, entered the Christian Brothers after burning his manuscripts in the manner of Gogol, devoted the remaining years of his life to teaching poor boys at North Monastery, Cork.

His play *Gissippus* which had failed to find acceptance during his lifetime produced at Drury Lane 1842, part of London just north of the Strand where signs saying, 'Beware of Sods!' were abundant.

When the boy was in the care of the Social Worker the rent boys of the Inner City would gather in all night cafés and speak a Polari, a cant of their own—a scatological cant.

One of them was found floating in a stone washed denim suit in the Liffey between Burgh Quay and Georges Quay. In one of those cafés there was an advertisement for

Wrangler Jeans on the wall: '*Let Wrangler lead you from the straight and narrow.*'

The *ragazzinos* from Sean McDermott Street, some of whom speak Polish now, fish in the Liffey for eel, mullet, crabs, using a rasher from Lidl as bait, which they fling in the Liffey when finished.

It was a tug of war between mother who loved the boy and wanted him back, to whom he'd run home last Christmas from the suburban orphanage and the House Father, Father, Social Worker, who wanted to adopt the boy, be father to son. The mother, the family, insisted there was a sexual element to the relationship.

In his flight from Ireland the Social Worker brought a photography album, photograph folder, loose photographs.

Were they Kodak photographs with white borders?

Naked, shorn of clothes, the boy was as pale, as pastel as the cuckoo flower—curvaceous too, a little Cupid, a little Amor.

In V-notch briefs white as a rabbit in a fox's mouth and after the summer his skin beige as the hares which sat on the golf course.

Naked, his penis and genitals were like the beige and nervous catkin of the hazel tree.

Naked, his body and penis were as white as the eggs of the wood pigeon, whose nest is a thin untidy platform of sticks in a tree or shrubs, his buttocks thin as the pigeon's untidy nest of sticks in a tree or shrubs.

Genitals like the ravishing bee-orchid with its pale purple Doge's hat above the bee-lip.

Nudity like the last snowdrops.

*'...make my grave both large and deep,
And my coffin of green birch.'*

'O younge Hugh of Lincoln! slain also With cursed Jewes!'

Little Saint Hugh of Lincoln, aged nine, disappeared July 31 1255, scourged, crowned with thorns, finally crucified, body found floating on water, hands and feet pierced with wounds, forehead lacerated. Buried near tomb of Robert Grosseteste, philosopher bishop of Lincoln.

Copin, a Jew, admitted murder under torture. He and eighteen other Jews hanged. Chaucer refers to Little Saint Hugh in *The Prioress' Tale*.

The golden haired subject of many screen paintings, twelve-year-old William of Norwich, skinner's apprentice who'd frequented the homes of Norwich's Jews, was found on Household Heath, Thorpe Wood, north east of Norman Norwich, which still exists, in March 1144. A one-eyed servant woman claimed she'd caught sight of the boy fastened to a post as she was bringing hot water to her Jewish master. Thorn points were found in the head, lacerations in the hands, feet, sides. Accusation that he was shaved, gagged, crucified were made against the Jews.

On February 6 1190 Norwich Jews who didn't manage to escape to Norwich Castle were slaughtered and this who escaped to the castle committed mass suicide.

Jews were expelled from England in 1290, many repatriated in Spain.

1492, after the Edict of Expulsion by Ferdinand and Isabella, the Jews of Segovia spent their last three days in the city in the Jewish Cemetery, fasting and lamenting over their dead.

'If his boyhood is reason enough for rejecting his holiness, we remind them of those boys Pancras... and Celsius.'

Pancras, a Phrygian orphan, was beheaded in Rome at the age of fourteen, his body covered in balsam by a Christian woman and buried in the Catacombs. Mentioned in Martyrology of Bede. Relics sent to Oswiu, King of Northumbria by Pope Vitalian around 664.

Celsus, a nine year old boy from Gaul, painted by Titian and Camillo Procaccini, was taken in a ship after Nero ordered him to be drowned, thrown overboard, but a storm arose, frightening the sailors, and he was pulled back on board. He was later beheaded in Milan.

Tarsicius, carrying the Eucharist to confessors in prison, and to Presbyters in other churches, was attacked by a pagan mob on the Appian Way with stones and clubs. Buried in the Cemetery of Callistus. He is the patron of altar boys.

The boy was altar boy age.

Skeletons found in the Tower of London 1674, are thought to be those of twelve-year-old Edward IV, a boy-child in ermine in an illumination in Lambeth Palace Library, and his younger brother, Richard, Duke of York, probably murdered on Richard III's instructions in the Tower, August 1483.

Gerda travelled to the palace of the Snow Queen with nothing to protect her but the Lord's Prayer... In the fourteenth century the bell maker of Breslau wanted to create his masterpiece for the Church of St. Mary Magdalen—the Sinner's Bell. In anger when his young boy apprentice interfered with the plug for the metals he stabbed him through the heart. For centuries, up to the end of the Second World

War, when the part of the church where the bell was situated was destroyed by explosion and fire, the Sinner's Bell tolled the Lord's Prayer.

In Medieval Christianity the Feast of the Holy Innocents was the last day of the Feast of Fools, last day young bishops had authority. In Medieval England boy-children were whipped naked in bed that morning, a custom which survived into the seventeenth century.

Perhaps the goose woman of Kassel had told the Brothers Grimm a version of *The Pied Piper of Hamelin*.

The Lueneberg Manuscript 1440-1450 states that in the year 1284 one hundred and thirty children of Hamelin were seduced by a piper in divers colours and murdered near the Koppen (Old German word for hills).

More likely it refers to the Children's Crusade—twelve-year-old Stephen of Cloyes who led thirty thousand children to the Mediterranean at Marseille, expecting it to part Nicholas, a ten-year-old shepherd from Cologne, who led twenty thousand children across the Alps, a loyal contingent of them to Genoa, where they were refused transport across the Mediterranean.

None of the children of the Children's Crusade ever reached Palestine. Many were taken as leaved to Tunisia. Many died in shipwrecks.

Norwich Jews who didn't manage to escape to Norwich Castle were murdered. A man's house is burned in Dundalk. A man's house burned in Newtown Mountkennedy, County Wicklow. A man's house is burned in Cavan and his cat burned alive.

A man is knifed in Donegal.

To go the way of the fox, another way, not their way. Tell the crows how beautiful they are and ask them to sing. Can a crow sing a folk-song? Can a crow tell a story?

> *'And I'll pike out his boony blue een,*
> *Wi'ae lock o his gowden hair,*
> *We'll theek aur nest*
> *When it grows bare.'*

Why does a fox cross the road? To get to the other side. I was never very good at jokes.

A boy said to his Mammy, 'Mammy, there's hair growing on my willy!'

'That's to keep you warm when you're swimming,' she said.

I was good at telling fairy stories. The fox will be out in an hour or two. To stroke you was like stroking the fox at evening.

There was an Irish Traveller in Glenochil called Maugham.

The Social Worker hung himself after ten years in the prison.

If you lose the narrative—the way the Little Mermaid lost her tongue and power of speech, the witch cutting her tongue out and then giving her a draught from a cauldron cleansed with snakes, sounding like a crocodile, one of the ingredients of which was her own black blood—you might as well be dead.

Hänsel reassures Gretel that God won't forsake them, finding their way home with the help of a duck.

Finding your way home.

Being in prison you miss the shelduck with beak red as war paint, black belly stripe from breast to vent, who nests in rabbit holes.

Being in prison is like going into the depths of a cave in Lascaux or Trois Frères to scratch a painting of a horse in bone or stone, hennaing the hide in, making it into fire, painting a human face—the soul of the horse. In prison you are scratching a picture of a boy-child in bone or stone on a prison wall, making his freckles and his hair into a fire.

Being in prison you miss the spring sunlight on the red brick Georgian houses of Buckingham Street, an inner city grimalkin-granny giving a wallop to a child in a red polka dot St. Vincent de Paul dress who refuses to be reproved.

Never again to see the early flowering cherry tree in first blossom beside St. Patrick's Cathedral.

Never again to see Wicklow saturated in primroses.

'Hello Mr Magpie, how do you do?
How is your wife and your children too?'

'I buried my own daughter,' a woman with crocheted white cap like a golf ball on her head tells me outside the ichorous—dried blood—Lourdes Church. 'She died of neurophagia. Aged three. They moved me out to Finglas after that. I stayed there three weeks. Then I came back to Sean McDermott Street.'

She remembers the boy's mother.

Harem scarum fringe, tuberous lips, baby girl with corkscrew fringe in her arms, blubber in her mouth.

'She lived in the tenements. There was Spanish blood somewhere.'

The smell of the tenement corridors, like a cardigan soaked in urine. And you were likely to encounter rats. Rats go for you. You get bitten on mouth. On ear. Rats and their legends were royal. Like the Georges under whose reign the houses were built. The railings were taken away 1932. Intercoms came late seventies.

'Rents were five shillings or seven and six. But they didn't have it.'

The moorhen has a roof I remember.

'Bailiffs parked cars at Garda Stations. They used catapults on them.

They burned floorboards to keep warm.'

And she spiels about namesakes of the boy's other but probably not her people.

'The grandmother lived on top of Mary's Mansions. The children used collect cabbage leaves, potato skins, hard bread on the balconies and bring them to her pigs. She had pigs in a shed in Hutton's Place behind the Bus Garage. They sold sea eels and salmon heads, Manx kippers and thornback ray on a stall in Parnell Street. Manx kippers were saltier. You had to soak the Manx kippers to get the dye out. They were up at five to buy the fish on Little Mary Street.

Maibe got a flat in Liberty House. It went on fire. She had windows locked because of the children. But the children weren't there. They tried to break her windows with a pick and couldn't. Even if they did the oxygen would have caused the flames to get worse. The place would have gone up in flames. She died, she did. It was the smoke.'

'You're a fucking nuisance,' a woman with hair arrangement like a boxing glove, in black and white, *langue-*

de-chat harem leggings, addresses her small child in its pram as she passes.

My informant diverges to namesakes of the boy's alcoholic father, probably not his people at all.

'They lived in Brigid's Mansions. Sheriff Street. Long knocked down. The eighties. The men were dockers. The women had stalls. Sold Dublin Bay prawns. Sold anything they could get their hands on. They'd sell yourself if you stood still. They were funny people. Had a sense of humour. You had to have. Some of them got Mickey money.'

(Compensation for alleged abuse in Industrial Schools.)

'There were Robin Hoods in those days. Commandos from the Second World War. They used catapults, ball-bearings, add traps with fishing tackle and clothes pegs for the Christian Brothers and Guards who came to take the boys away.'

As slave ships sailed up rivers in West Africa in the eighteenth century so young strawberry faced guards went into Sean McDermott Street, picked up boys, sent them to Industrial Schools, where they sought the warmth of the chapels as the pied wagtails sought the warmth of the Christmas lights on the plane trees on O'Connell Street.

'There was one fellow who was in Artane for stealing. He was kicked to death. The mother went to the Brother and asked for money for the burial. The Brother said he could be buried in Artane. The mother got a hire purchase coffin. He was buried in a pauper's grave in Glasnevin.

There was a man who was in an Industrial School and he married a woman who was in an Industrial School. They had six children. Both walked down the steps into the Liffey.'

A stocky mother passes holding hand of a daughter with Down Syndrome, the girl's hair clubbed at the back by black embroidery. She has ear plugs. Her stride is springy.

'I better hurry on. I'll miss me Lotto.

Go and see the priest.'

The priest's cardigan is ash grey but his eyes are the green of tartan bartered in the Atlantic towns of Mayo, a little of Stuart Hunting green.

'There were millers down the docks. The dockers had slash hooks, machetes to pull cargo. Containers came in 1965. The dockers were laid off.

When the 1970s came some of the youths got high power rifles, some hunting rifles. Some joined the Republican Movement. Some turned to crime. Some to heroin. Heroin came in the seventies.'

A bedlam of boys from Mary Mansions attack me with snowballs.

'Leave him alone,' says one with hair the colour of crusts of Brennan's sliced bread.

'Stop that,' comes the megaton accent of a woman sitting like a Buddha on front of a basket of plastic lustre flowers and some tchotchkes at one of the windows of Mary Mansions.

'I'm writing a poem about my dog now,' a woman wearing glasses with blue frames, with a lantern chin, a Dutch cut, carrying a handbag with a pattern of mallards in all kinds of states—swimming, standing, flying, spreading their wings—tells me outside Lourdes Church. 'My last poem was about my friend who died in an orphanage in Wicklow.

Saturday night was writing night in the orphanage.

We ran away once and went to Bray.

We'd heard there was a call girl in Bray aged forty-two.

We had fish and chips in Papa Lino's. We rode the golden gallopers. We had chips in the Capri before we went back.

She used always come into my dormitory from her dormitory at night and whisper in my ear.

One night she didn't come in and I went looking for her and she was dead.'

'Pillycock, pillycock, sate on a hill
If he's not gone—he sits there still.'

'I can smell the shite off you!' Says a boy who looks like a balloon blown up, with a Dublin accent coming out of a balloon, to a boy with hair the autobiography of a fox, outside Lourdes Church.

'Two seconds to go and it's on me knickers.'

In almost uniform tracksuits the youths look like an army. People at war. Sean McDermott Street is an ordinance survey, a map of war.

Thornback ray...

Vietnamese, Chinese, Thai, takeaway fronts say now. There's been a 'Dog found' notice in marker on one of their windows for years.

Boys dart out of sidestreets near the takeaways at dusk like nightjars, the bicycles making a sound like the Irish name for nightjars—*Tuine Lín* (flax spinning wheel). Nightjars were the púca bird.

'Sweet Pucke, You do their works, and they shall haue good luck.'

A dwarf in a T-shirt with a reclining girl in stocking boots, drawstring bikini, passes with a poodle on a leash.

A man in a wheelchair wearing a Stars baseball hat with Stripes under the peak.

A man in a blue-grey T-shirt with a grey snarling hare's head on it, the hare's mouth outlined in scarlet, emerges from a sex shop.

"Is that a hare?' someone asked me, 'Only a pubic hare,' I told him.'

'In this part of Dublin cousins go with cousins and brothers with brothers. I went with thirteen year olds. Is there anything wrong with that?

At ten they played with one another. The older ones brought the younger ones home, played Kings and Queens. Ten year olds were the Queens. Had to strip. Lie on the bed.

It was common for fathers to have sex with sons. Sometimes the fathers would have sex with sons when they were six.

A man tried to have sex with Waldi Handiside when he was fourteen and when he wouldn't go along with him the man hung him from a rowan tree the Corporation put there. Passersby cut him down and saved his life.

There was a gang rape then by a gang on Sean McDermott Street. Umbrella up vagina. Nipples cut off. The girl died.'

Sean McDermott Street boys in prison got prison tattoos—biro and ink, thread around ballpoint—of swifts on their wrists. No legs, tiny feet.

The swifts returned beginning of May—clung to the Georgian walls with their tiny feet. When on the wing approach their nests, bang on them with a wing, without landing.

Began return journey to Africa beginning of August.

And the man finishes: 'I started putting on my mother's stretch satin mini panties when I was twelve. At fourteen staying with my aunt on Tonlagee Road she caught me in her mini-length silk slip. She was very understanding.

She was a Ladybird.'

I look in the mirror to see where she lives now.

'Mirror, Mirror, on the wall, who in this land is the fairest of all?'

A woman passes us in fuschine mules and dressing gown, with a tan from California Sun in Ballybough.

Edenmore. Donnycarney Church. Darndale. Oscar Traynor Road. Tonlagee Road. St. Margaret's Estate. Popintree.

You move to these parts but it's a way of seeing things, a way of being alive.

You miss the insomniac swifts.

You miss the funerals with the piper with the pony tail, sleeper in ear, black covert coat, crocus-gold kilt who leads the corteges with a coronoch of pipes, women pulling on cigarettes as they await the arrival of the hearse and coffin.

You miss the streets Matt Talbot walked on with chain on waist, chain on one arm, on the other arm a cord, a chain below the kneecap of one leg.

You miss the thornback ray.

'A woman stayed on ten years after they tried to move her out. Fourth floor Foley Street.

(Legion of Mary cleaned it up in the 1920s.)

Eight flights of steps up. With only the light of the Fiesta Club, Talbot Street, or the security lights of Ruttles Clothes factory.

She got tinnitus from the noise of the night club.

A neighbour brought an electric stove. She had no water. Youths would have rocket fuel (cider) parties at night. They came with jack hammers on the roof and threw things down.

The pubs were closed. The neighbours gone. She died of a broken heart.'

The legends of Wicklow where the little boy spent his last months, having run away from the suburban city orphanage, back to his mother: the raven, spilt Saint Kevin of Glendalough's milk when he was a boy and Saint Kevin cursed them and they couldn't land on his Feast Day June 3 or get food—they had to rely on their caches of food under rocks or crevices; an otter brought Saint Kevin salmon for his nascent community; a black bird hatched her blue-green, finely brown speckled egg, on his outstretched hand as he prayed.

A three-year-old boy had been scalded to death in a hot bath in this orphanage in 1947.

A panavision family of foxes lived nearby.

Early March the blanket of snowdrops on the lawn became like a handkerchief someone had cried into.

The sharp rush—*an luachair bhiorach*—large, pointed tips, grew on the nearby coast, where there was a strip of clandestine beach, white as monastic voyager's sails.

There was a brother and sister in the area in their sixties who were having sex with one another. He wore a tea caddy on his head.

The orphanage was burned down purposely end of the eighties. A Vocational School, an old building, was also burned down, same way, about 1995.

A Church of Ireland rector was stabbed to death during a night robbery.

When a man has had a sexual relationship with a very young boy, sometimes in love-making, the boy has been accidentally killed—strangled usually, asphyxiated.

The yellow and black striped caterpillar becomes a tortoiseshell butterfly with hind wings which have dark margins towards the body containing bright blue crescents. Towards late summer—when the Social Worker from the suburban city orphanage collected the boy in Wicklow orphanage, after the boy had run away to him a few times— the tortoiseshell butterfly basks as long as possible on meadow trails or sea trails, clasping the earth with its wings, to absorb as much heat as possible to prolong its life.

'Why are people attracted to pre-pubescent boys?' you ask.

'It's the moment,' is the answer. 'Some of those who are say their father were like that before them. It runs in the family.

It's also about control. You can control.'

Control.

End the life of a nine-year-old boy.

Some of those Brothers were like Pygmalion, a King of Cyprus, father of Adonis, who carved an ivory statue and then fell in love with his creation, the Goddess Venus bringing the statue to life, or like Geppetto the Woodcarver who carved Pinocchio from a piece of pine. The altar boys, the nine year olds with catechism bodies, were statues or wood carvings brought to life.

'Some priests, Brothers were too shy for thirteen and fourteen year olds. Thirteen and fourteen was too old.'

Did the Social Worker give a birthday card to the boy on his ninth birthday, his final birthday with Arthur Rackham's *Old Woman Who Lived Under a Hill* on it —an old lady in a witch's hat, skirt patterned with pink flowers and apple green foliage, zebra-striped cat beside her?

The hour of the Witch...

Hänsel and Gretel managed to shove the cannibalistic witch into the oven in which she'd planned to roast them.

In a London guest house did they sleep together under a bedspread patterned with a soccer player and the same soccer player on the purple pillows?

The frog managed to get into the Royal bed.

But the princess threw the frog against the wall in disgust and he became a prince.

To the grey Georgian brick of Edinburgh against the red Georgian brick of Dublin.

The dying Little Match Girl lit a match on New Year's Eve, which made the wall she was lying against transparent, and saw a Christmas tree with thousands of candles on its branches, the ultimate candles becoming stars which took her to death.

A bath in an Edinburgh Hotel.

The bath in Marlborough House on Washerwoman's Lane was sexual folklore.

Erections at nine the way Pinocchio's nose grows larger when he's lying, pubes at ten.

To trace the vines of the everlasting pea in the dunes until you come to pink flower like a small boy's genitals.

Snowdrops become ghosts in the grass in March.

It wasn't murder, it was a mixture of horseplay as he said, and sexual play.

The Social Worker took an overdose after the boy drowned. 'It is just a pity it didn't work for me,' he told the police.

I like solitary and rare birds like the yellow wagtail who peruses the seaside streams.

We live in a world where the Slave Aesop's goose has been murdered. There are no more golden eggs, no more dreams, no more running away.

Appendix

22-23 *The Flamarion*, fom Camille Flammarion's *L'atmosphère: météorologie populaire* (1888), Artist unknown. Public domain

44 *The Fuse*, from *The City* comic, © Stephen Crowe 2013. Reproduced with the artist's permission

72 *Isms*, from *The City* comic, © Stephen Crowe 2013. Reproduced with the artist's permission

114 *A Brand New Axe*, from *The City* comic, © Stephen Crowe 2013. Reproduced with the artist's permission

124 *Vagues* was originally written for The European Short Story Network: www.theshortstory.eu

152 Portrait of Alberto Giacometti, 1961 © Henri Cartier-Bresson/ Magnum Photos. Courtesy of Magnum Photos

161 Portrait of Avigdor Arikhah, 1985. © Henri Cartier-Bresson/ Magnum Photos. Courtesy of Magnum Photos

169 *Not From Around Here*, from *The City* comic, © Stephen Crowe 2013. Reproduced with the artist's permission

197 *12 Angry Films*, 2006 © Jesse Jones. Image courtesy the artist

216 Still from *The Other North,* 2013 © Jesse Jones. Image courtesy the artist

223 *There Isn't Much Time Now*, from *The City* comic, © Stephen Crowe 2013. Reproduced with the artist's permission

Contributors

DARRAN ANDERSON is an Irish writer. His 33 1/3 book on Serge Gainsbourg's *Histoire de Melody Nelson* has been published by Bloomsbury in 2013. His Borges and Calvino-inspired book *Imaginary Cities* and his critical study of the novels of Jack Kerouac are due to be published by Influx Press and Reaktion Books respectively in 2014.

ANNA ASLANYAN is a journalist and translator. She writes for a number of publications—including *3:AM Magazine, TLS, The Independent* and *The National*—mainly on books and arts. Among her translations into Russian are works by Peter Ackroyd, John Berger, Tom McCarthy, Jeffrey Eugenides and Zadie Smith. Her translations from Russian into English include contemporary short stories and a collection of essays *Post-Post Soviet? Art, Politics and Society in Russia at the Turn of the Decade*.

KEVIN BREATHNACH is the literary editor of *Totally Dublin*. His work has also appeared in *The New Inquiry, The Stinging Fly, The Quarterly Conversation* and *3:AM Magazine*. He currently lives in Dublin.

STEPHEN CROWE is a British illustrator based in Seattle. Since 2009 he's been illustrating *Finnegans Wake* for a project called *Wake in Progress*. His new comic, *The City*, which he updates irregularly online, follows the misadventures of a large cast of characters in an unnamed European capital amid the turmoil following the First World War.

ROB DOYLE's fiction, essays and reviews have appeared in *The Dublin Review, The Stinging Fly, The Moth* and elsewhere. His writing has been translated into French and Serbian. His first novel, *Here are the Young Men*, will be published in May 2014 by the Lilliput Press. Rob holds a Masters from Trinity College Dublin, where he studied Philosophy and Psychoanalysis. Born in Dublin in 1982, he is currently living in Rosslare, County Wexford.

CONTRIBUTORS

S.J. FOWLER is a poet, artist, martial artist & vanguardist. He works in the modernist and avant-garde traditions, across poetry, fiction, sonic art, visual art, installation and performance. He has published five books and been commissioned by the Tate, Mercy, *Penned in the Margins* and the London Sinfonietta. He is the poetry editor of *3:AM Magazine* and is the curator of the Enemies project.

DAVID GAVAN was educated in London and currently lives in County Meath, Ireland. He has written for the *Irish Examiner*, *Time Out*, *Record Collector*, *AU* magazine and *The Quietus*. He is co-editor of *gorse*.

COLIN HERD is a poet, fiction writer and critic. His first collection of poems *too ok* was published by BlazeVOX in 2011. A pamphlet, *like*, was published by Knives, Forks and Spoons Press in 2011 and a second full-length collection, *Glovebox & Other Poems*, in 2013. He lives in Edinburgh.

DESMOND HOGAN is the author of five novels, *The Ikon-Maker*, *The Leaves on Grey*, *A Curious Street*, *A New Shirt* and *A Farewell to Prague*, and ten short story collections, most recently *The House of Mourning & Other Stories* (Dalkey Archive Press 2013).

JOHN HOLTEN's first novel *The Readymades* was published in 2011 by Broken Dimanche Press. His second, *Oslo, Norway*, is due for publication in 2014. www.johnholten.com

MATTHEW JAKUBOWSKI's fiction has been published by *3:AM Magazine*, *Fiddleblack*, *Corium*, and *Necessary Fiction*. He is an editor for *Asymptote*, a journal of world literature, and lives with his wife and son in Philadelphia.

RICHARD KOVITCH is a writer and director based in London whose work has won awards in Europe and the USA. His feature documentary *Penelope Slinger—An Exorcism* is due for release in 2014.

JULIE REVERB is a London-based torch singer turned writer. Her work has appeared in *3:AM Magazine*, *Sleepingfish* and *Squawk Back*. Her debut novella will be published later this year. www.juliereverb.com

SUSAN TOMASELLI is the editor of *gorse*. She has written for the *Guardian*, *The Stinging Fly*, *3:AM Magazine* and elsewhere. She lives in Dublin.

JOANNA WALSH's work has been published by Tate, *Granta*, *London Review of Books*, *n+1*, *The Guardian*, *The White Review*, *Narrative Magazine*, and *The European Short Story Network*. Her collection of short stories, *Fractals*, is published by 3:AM Press. She is also an illustrator, and has also created large scale drawings for The Tate Modern and The Wellcome Institute.

KARL WHITNEY lives in Sunderland and is working on a non-fiction book about Dublin, to be published by Penguin Ireland.

DAVID WINTERS writes literary criticism, and co-edits *3:AM Magazine*. He has contributed to the *TLS*, the *Guardian*, the *Independent*, *Radical Philosophy* and elsewhere.

Friends of gorse

We would like to acknowledge the generous involvement of the following individuals:

Kevin Barry
Robert Brown
J. Fusco
Tammy Ho Lai-Ming
David Minogue
Jason O'Rourke
Colm O'Shea
Amanda L. Phillips
Rrose Sélavy
Michael N. Shanks
Jon K. Shaw

And those who wish to remain anonymous.

If you wish to support *gorse*, please visit:
www.gorse.ie